# How to Find
## the
# Right Pastor

*Dr. Larry A. Maxwell*

# How to Find
## the
# Right Pastor

## A Biblical Perspective
## & Comprehensive Manual

by

Dr. Larry A. Maxwell

*Dedicated to two outstanding men of God who had a lasting influence on my life and taught me so much about Pastoral ministry: my Pastor, Dr. Jerry Falwell, and my Pastoral Theology Professor, Dr. C. Sumner Wemp.*

Dr. Jerry Falwell          Dr. C. Sumner Wemp

# Published by Challenge International

**Southern Tier New York Office:**
1130 Perry Rd., Afton, New York 13730
**Patterson, New York Office:**
599 Route 311, Patterson, New York 12563
Website: GoodInformation.US

ISBN-13: 978-1499713411
ISBN-10: 149971341X

Cover Design & Photo by Matthew Reid Maxwell

Many portions of this book were part of the *How to Find the Right Pastor Notebook* originally copyrighted by this author in 1987.
Images of Dr. Falwell and Dr. Wemp are from www.Liberty.edu
All Scripture Quotations are from the King James Version (KJV).

# Table of Contents

*Dr. Larry A. Maxwell*

# Introduction

Every week, churches all around the world are seeking a new Pastor. Finding the *Right Pastor* is a serious task. It is often a complex and emotionally wrenching experience, which will have an effect on everyone in a church.

Some churches belong to denominations, associations or fellowships, which provide assistance finding a Pastor, but many churches, must pursue this task on their own.

Pastors take courses in college and seminary covering subject matter such as, *How to Find the Right Church*, and, *Candidating and Accepting a Pastorate*. How many laypeople ever take a course entitled, *How to Find the Right Pastor?*

Over the years, I saw many churches struggle trying to find the *Right Pastor*. As I assisted many in their search, I designed these materials to provide practical help and guidance for churches looking to find the *Right Pastor*. I say *Right Pastor*, because many churches know what it is like to find the *Wrong Pastor* and do not want to repeat that experience.

This book should be a helpful tool for *any church* seeking a Pastor, regardless of their denomination or beliefs. Much of this material can also help a synagogue find the *Right Rabbi*.

Churches with diametrically opposite belief systems have successfully used these materials. If you believe the Bible is the inspired, infallible, inerrant Word of God, this book will help you find a like-minded Pastor. Yet, if you do not believe that, you can use these materials to make sure your Prospective Pastor holds to what you believe.

One very important aspect of this book is it helps your church identify what you believe. That is very important to help you find a Pastor who is compatible with your church.

The Bible lists qualifications for a Pastor *(you may agree with that, you may not)*, but the big challenge is, it does not specifically say *how* or *where* to find the *Right Pastor*.

Finding the *Right Pastor* is a unique task with unique criteria. Some churches mistakenly treat the search for a Pastor as if they are a company looking for a new employee. It is quite different from that. The task of finding the *Right Pastor* is more like a company looking for a new president, with a number of significant differences. It has more similarities to someone looking for a spouse.

This book sets out important criteria and suggested guidelines your church should prayerfully consider as they search for the *Right Pastor* God has for you.

This manual, and the task before you, may seem overwhelming. You are embarking on a serious challenge, but do not despair. Ask God for wisdom (James 1:5), then proceed. Know you can do all things through Christ who will strengthen you if you ask Him (Philippians 4:13). Taking the time to put in the extra effort suggested in this manual, and doing the task correctly is better than taking what appears to be an easier road and finding yourself having to do it all over again.

If you have any questions about the process or need any assistance, please feel free to contact me. Part of my ministry is providing administrative assistance to local churches.

## Editor's Notes

The Greek Text used is the *Received Text* also referred to as the *Textus Receptus*. Greek words are transliterated *(English characters are substituted for the Greek letters)*.

Numerous words in this book are Captilized or *Italicized*, or **Both**, for emphasis.

# The Romantic Parallel

There are a number of similarities between the process a Pastoral Search Committee goes through to find a Pastor and the process of looking for a spouse. Understanding those parallels can add a new dimension to the search for the *Right Pastor*.

In the 1960's there was a television show called, *The Dating Game*. On that show, one person interviewed three prospective dating candidates. Based on their responses, that person selected one of those three for a date.

Many Pastoral Search Committees operate very similar to *The Dating Game*. The *Pastoral Search Game* lines up potential prospects and decides which one they will select to be their Candidate. It is interesting to note, out of the 2,035 episodes of *The Dating Game,* not one of the resulting couples ever married each other and lived happily ever after. It does not work very well for those who play *The Pastoral Search Game* either.

Some churches conduct their Pastoral Search like two other television shows, *The Bachelor* or *The Bachelorette*. On those shows, a series of eligible potential spouses interact in an ongoing competition, eliminating one after another until only one remains to become Mr. or Mrs. Right.

Both of those methods are very far from the Biblical Model for courtship and even further, away from the proper procedure a church should follow when seeking a Pastor.

The following are the steps involved in developing a lasting, meaningful, romantic relationship. Notice the parallels between that and finding the *Right Pastor*.

## 1.    Identify Someone.

If you want a long-term, meaningful, romantic relationship, you must look for one special person. You must be purposefully looking or they will pass you by. In your search, you will inevitably see many nice people. It may take a while before one will grab your attention and makes your heart beat faster.

If someone catches your attention, in a special way, you will want to know more about them. Two of the most important pieces of information you will seek to find out are their name and if they are in a serious relationship. You will have many questions. It is very likely you will ask other people questions about that person. If you know people who know that person well, those are the best sources for that preliminary information. Many people do an internet search to see what pops up about that person.

It is interesting to note many successful relationships are inaugurated by one person introducing two people to each other.

In the same manner, a Pastoral Search Committee must look for a Potential Candidate. A *Pastoral Candidate Recommendation Form* is very helpful for that. Other people use that form to introduce you to Potential Candidates, whom they recommend. That form also provide answers to some important questions.

## 2.    The First Date.

In the Romantic Parallel, once you identify someone who interests you, you must take the initiative and approach him or her. If they respond well, you ask them out on a first date.

Could you imagine if you approached someone, you were interested in, and said to them,

> *I am looking for a potential spouse whom I will love and cherish with all my heart. Right now, I am trying to narrow down the field, so I am setting up some dates with a few potential prospects and would like to take you out on a date so I can see if you meet my expectations.*

With that technique, it is unlikely you would ever get a first date. The sad thing is that is very similar to how some Pastoral Search Committees operate.

If you properly approach someone, they may agree to go on that first date with you. That first date is very important. Sometimes all it takes is one date to learn someone is not the right person for you, or on that first date, you can discover there may be the possibility for a lasting relationship.

After that first date, each person individually determines if they are interested in pursuing the relationship. That does not mean they are making a commitment, it just means they are interested in taking the steps to get to know each other better.

In the same way, a Pastoral Search Committee must make that first contact and get together with a Prospective Candidate. That first contact is so important. The person may say yes or no. If the Prospective Candidate expresses an interest, both parties need to get together, face to face. That personal meeting will help both the Pastoral Search Committee and Prospective Candidate determine if they want to proceed any further.

## 3.    Becoming a Couple.

After a few dates, a couple usually gets to know each other better. Then, one or the other, or both of them, decide to stop pursing one another, or decide to continue the relationship.

If the two parties decide to continue the relationship, from that point, they often begin to identify themselves to others as a *couple*. During that time, they only date one another while they learn more and more about each other.

Though most people do not specifically state this, the purpose of dating is to determine long-term compatibility. Some people can have many areas of compatibility, which is perfect for a good friendship, but not for a marriage. In the same way, the Pastoral Search Committee and Church must determine if they and the Prospective Candidate appear to be compatible for a long-term relationship. In many cases, some learn it would be better to be just friends. If the church believes there is the possibility of long-term compatibility, they vote to invite the Prospect to become their Candidate so they can officially take the next steps get to know each other better.

## 4.    Getting Engaged.

As a couple spends more time together, they have conversations about what they like, and more deeper conversations about who they are. They share their hopes and dreams and intimate details about themselves. After a while, as they get to know each other better, they determine if they are compatible and interested in a serious long-term relationship. If they decide they might be better just being friends, they should break off the relationship. On the other hand, if they believe they do have the compatibility to become a married couple, they enter into a formal engagement.

In the Pastoral Search process, there are three parties involved; the Pastoral Search Committee, the Church and the Candidate. They all need to get to know each other better. They need to understand each other's hopes and dreams and share intimate details. During that process, as they get to know each other better, they must determine if they have some significant differences and are not compatible. If that is the case, then they should amicably break off that relationship. On the other hand, if they determine they are compatible, then the Church should extend the call to the Candidate to become their Pastor.

## 5.    The Engagement Period.

Once a couple decides to be engaged, they enter the engagement period of their relationship. Many people incorrectly assume that guarantees they are going to get married. Sometimes that is not the case. The purpose of the engagement period is for a couple to *seek to work out the details* to see if they can agree on the specifics for their marriage and future life together. Some couples discover they cannot work out those details and break off their engagement. That is a good thing. That is much better than being like many couples who do not properly address those details, get married and then things do not work out and they go through the intense pain of a failing marriage.

In the same way, after a church extends a call to a Candidate to become their Pastor, the church and the Candidate need to negotiate all the details, such as a compensation package, before the call is officiated. Many times that works out, but there are times that it does not work out. If they cannot work out the details, then they need to end the relationship.

## 6.     The Wedding.

After a couple works out all the details, then their Wedding Ceremony takes place. It is at the Wedding they legally become husband and wife and their marriage begins. After that, if they both work at it, they will have a wonderful, long lasting meaningful relationship.

In the same way, a Pastoral Search Committee and a Candidate must come to an agreement on all the details, and then schedule a *Pastoral Installation Service*. The Installation Service is a time of celebration. It is at that service, the Candidate officially becomes Pastor of the Church. After that, if both parties work at it, they will have a wonderful, long lasting relationship.

*Dr. Larry A. Maxwell*

# Form a Pastoral Search Committee

## Step 1.

### Determine Who Decides Who Fills the Pulpit, Before You Form This Committee.

There are many questions and issues to address when a church is without a Pastor. The first thing you must do, even before forming a Pastoral Search Committee, is make sure someone is scheduled to preach for your services.

Scheduling people to fill the pulpit is a very important task. People will assume the people who fill the pulpit are presenting a message endorsed by your church. You must be very careful who you have fill the pulpit.

Some churches decide to save money and have some of their own people fill the pulpit. Though there are times, when it can be appropriate for some laypeople to preach, that is not the Biblical model for sustained pulpit ministry. God specifically calls some people to be Pastors. Do not set off on the wrong foot. Your goal should be to have the pulpit filled by people God called to a pulpit ministry.

Some **Church Constitutions and By-Laws** specify who is responsible to schedule the speakers to fill the pulpit. If those documents do not assign that task, I recommend you assign that task to the Deacons, if you have some. If you do not have Deacons, then you should assign this task to the Church Board. Do not entrust the Pastoral Search Committee with the task of filling the pulpit, except when they are scheduling approved Candidates, as that presents a conflict of interest.

## Three Important Stipulations for Filling the Pulpit:

1. **Those Who *Fill* the Pulpit should NOT be Prospective Candidates for Pastor.**
2. **The Deacons should Consider Suggestions for Pulpit Supply from the Congregation.**
3. **The Pastoral Search Committee's Scheduling of Candidates, Supersedes Pre-scheduled Speakers.**

Unlike regular speakers, who may speak in your church at other times, those you schedule to *fill* the pulpit, when you are seeking a Pastor, should do so with the understanding they are not being considered as a Candidate. They also need to understand you may need to cancel or postpone their speaking engagement if you need to have a Prospective Candidate or Candidate speak. Try to give a pulpit supply speaker at least two weeks' notice if you need to cancel them.

It is best to try to have a full pulpit schedule one to two months in advance. Things will come up, and you may have to make some schedule changes but those who can fill the pulpit, and do a good job, usually plan ahead at least a few months or longer.

It is a good idea to keep records of sermon titles the speakers use in your pulpit and provide those, in advance, to those filling the pulpit. This is not essential but you will be pleased if you do this and do not have the same sermon topic for five out of seven weeks.

Be sure you have a **Compensation Plan** *(addressed later in this book)* in place for those filling the pulpit.

# Step 2.
# Consider Selecting an Interim Pastor.

In many cases, it is wise to consider calling someone to serve as an Interim Pastor to fulfill the Pastoral duties in your church during the process of finding the *Right Pastor*.

Calling an Interim Pastor is especially helpful if your church has gone through a bad experience surrounding the leaving of your former Pastor. In that case, it may be advisable to call an Interim Pastor and wait to form a Pastoral Search Committee temporarily for a specific time, such as six months. After that specific time has elapsed, the church should vote to either form the Pastoral Search Committee or postpone that until another date. It is still a good idea to have the Interim Pastor continue to serve until you call a new Pastor.

## 1.  The Purpose & Qualifications for an Interim Pastor.

You may have one or two primary speakers who speak regularly during your Pastoral Search but there is other Pastoral work, someone needs to do, other than just filling the pulpit. The purpose of an Interim Pastor is not just to fill the pulpit but also to provide a *Transitional Shepherd* for the flock.

An Interim Pastor should generally be an older experienced minister who has Pastoral experience but who either is retired or serves specifically as an Interim Pastor to help churches in transition.

You should check with any associations or fellowships you belong to for recommendations for someone to serve as in Interim Pastor. Make sure they come highly recommended

In some areas with a seminary, Bible College, or other large ministry nearby, some professors or staff are available to serve as Interim Pastors.

## 2.  The Duties & Term of an Interim Pastor.

You should call an Interim Pastor to serve for a specific limited time, preferably in six-month increments. Before their term expires, your church should conduct a review to see if it should extend that term for an additional six-month increment.

The Interim Pastor should fulfill most of the duties and responsibilities of a Pastor. That could include hospital visitation for members, counselling the bereaved, conducting funerals and weddings as well as any other Pastoral duties you specify.

You may agree there will be certain Pastoral duties he shall not fulfill. If your Pastor sits as a member or ex-officio member on any church board or committee, it would be a good idea for the Interim Pastor to attend those meeting. He could give Pastoral input at those meetings, but it would probably be a good idea that he would not have the vote your Pastor would.

### 3.    What to Pay an Interim Pastor.

You should pay an Interim Pastor the equivalent salary and benefits as a regular Pastor, for the duties he performs, minus housing, retirement and health benefits.

Most churches have the Trustees, who are the legal and financial representatives of the church; negotiate the details of salary and benefits and then present it to your church for approval. Their responsibilities include overseeing and managing the church finances so this usually falls under their jurisdiction.

### 4.    Negative Aspect of an Interim Pastor.

One of the negative aspects of having an Interim Pastor is some churches, especially smaller churches, can become comfortable and complacent, having an Interim Pastor, and put off the Pastoral Search. The Interim Pastor should help make sure that does not happen.

# Step 3.
# Establish a Pastoral Search Committee.

### 1.    Determine Who Will Serve on the Pastoral Search Committee.

The next thing you need to do, to find the *Right Pastor*, is to establish a Pastoral Search Committee. The Pastoral Search

Committee acts on behalf of the Church in screening, contacting and interviewing Prospective Candidates for the position of Pastor.

Most often, a **Church's Constitution and By-Laws** addresses this procedure. If such a procedure is not spelled out in your Constitution and By-Laws, the Church should appoint a committee with a minimum of three (3) mature Christians to act as the Pastoral Search Committee. It is wise to set a maximum of no more than six (6) members. Do not make the Pastoral Search Committee too large or it will be too hard to get everyone together for a meeting.

Some churches have the Deacons and sometimes the Trustees make up this Committee. That is not a good idea. The Pastoral Search Committee needs a broader representation from the Church Body. If you have Deacons and Trustees, I recommend you let each group select a representative, from among themselves, to be included on the Committee.

Make sure this Committee represents the various groups in your church. It is a good idea to have someone represent the Women of the Church, as well as one to represent the Senior Saints and one to represent the Young People. If you have a significant presence of any Ethnic groups, Deaf or Singles *(or single again)*, I recommend having them represented either as members of the Committee or advisors to the Committee.

Remember the Pastor, which the Committee recommends will become the Pastor of everyone in the church, if approved.

Each member of the Pastoral Search Committee should be a member of the church, in good standing, who actively participates in all aspects of the life of the church. They should be a faithful financial supporter of the church and be in complete agreement with the **Church's Constitution, By Laws** and **Doctrinal Statement**. In addition, they should have a vibrant personal and public walk with God and a good testimony with their family and community. They should also be a person of prayer, as well as one who is willing, and able, to work with others on this important task.

## 2. Assign Responsibilities to Committee Members.

To have an effective Pastoral Search Committee it is important to select a *Chairman* and *Secretary*.

Assign responsibilities to the Chairman and Secretary and to each member of the Committee.

Every duty of the Pastoral Search Committee is important. Make sure you assign responsibilities to people who are willing and capable to perform their duties.

### Chairman of the Pastoral Search Committee.

O    The Chairman shall serve as moderator and motivator for the Pastoral Search Committee.

O    The Chairman shall regularly report the activities of the Pastoral Search Committee to the Church.

### Secretary of the Pastoral Search Committee.

O    The Secretary shall keep minutes of all Pastoral Search Committee Meetings.

O    The Secretary shall send correspondence to possible Candidates and maintain a record of all correspondence sent and received.

### Assign the Following Specific Responsibilities to People on the Committee:

O    Someone to Contact Sources for Candidates.

O    Someone to Receive Recommendations.

O    Someone to Arrange Travel, Meals and Housing for Candidates.

O    Someone to Check References.

O    Someone to Serve as the Phone Contact for Candidates.

# Step 4.
# Determine the Church's Official Procedure for Considering & Calling a Candidate.

The Pastoral Search Committee must identify and determine the Church's **Procedure for Considering & Calling a Candidate**. As a legal entity, it is important to have an Officially Approved Procedure to follow. Often, official church documents or records do not contain an official procedure for considering and calling a Candidate.

Some churches put together an official set of **Policies and Procedures**, addressing practical operational items for the ministry, separate from their **Constitution** and **By-Laws**. This is wise because, in a world with accelerated technological changes and rapidly changing socio-economic factors, operational policies and procedures are more fluid and need to be able to change more readily.

**Understand the Following Distinctions:**

O    The **Church Constitution** is a founding document, which sets forth the *purpose* and *foundational beliefs* of an organization. It should be difficult to change.

Here is an example of a *purpose* a church Constitution could address. It could say, *the church shall conduct worship services*. If it says you should conduct Sunday Morning Worship Services, and something happens to prevent you from conducting a Sunday Morning Service, your church could be subjected to a lawsuit and the possibility of being legally disbanded. Be careful what you are specific about in your Constitution. Remember you are stating *purposes* **not** *specifics of how you carry out those purposes*.

In relation to the Pastoral Search, a **Church Constitution** can say the Church shall have a Pastor and list certain qualifications for the Pastor.

○ The **Church By-Laws** are a founding document which set forth some of the *operational purposes* of the organization. They should not address the day-to-day operational specifics. By-Laws should be easier to change than the Constitution.

Here is an example the By-Laws could address. It should say, *if possible, the church should have a weekly worship service each Sunday.* It should not say Sunday *Morning* or a specific time. You may end up in a situation where you need to meet on a Sunday afternoon. It is better to put specifics you can change in your **Official Procedures**.

In relation to the Pastoral Search, the **Church By-Laws** may say how you choose a Pastoral Search Committee and list some general duties.

○ The **Official Procedures** spell out specific operational procedures a church shall follow. These should be even easier to change than the By-Laws.

Here is an example of an operational procedure. It could say *the church shall conduct a weekly Sunday Morning Service at 10:30 a.m.*

In relation to the Pastoral Search, the **Official Procedures** can spell out the specific procedure a Pastoral Search Committee should follow.

This book provides a **Suggested Procedure for Considering and Calling a Candidate** in a later section. You may want to look at that now.

○ The **Official Policies** spell out specific details to accompany the Procedure. Often the Procedures and Policies are combined in one document or manual. These should be easy to change.

In relation to the Pastoral Search, the **Official Policies** should include specific policies, such as are suggested in this section of this book.

# Step 5.
# Determine Official Policies.

The Pastoral Search Committee serves as representatives of the church. They must follow the *Procedures* (the road map) established by the church for finding a new Pastor and act within the *Policies* (the specific details and directions) determined by the church.

If *Official Polices* are not set forth in the official records of the church, the Pastoral Search Committee should address the following tasks, preferably in the order presented here:

### 1.    Find Some Godly Pastors to Serve as Advisors.

The Bible says there is safely in the multitude of counselors (Proverbs 11:14; 15:22; 24:6). It is a wise decision for a Pastoral Search Committee to ask some Pastors, whom your church respects to serve as advisors. They can provide invaluable wisdom and guidance.

### 2.    Recommend Policies for the Church to Officially Adopt.

Besides having an **Official Procedure** to follow, each church needs to have **Official Policies** for the Pastoral Search Committee to follow when for seeking and calling a new Pastor. If such policies do not exist, the Pastoral Search Committee should prayerfully draft Recommended Policies *(such as suggested here)* and then present them to the Church to review and vote upon before those policies become Official Church Policy. It is very important for every church to have Official Policies and Procedures.

When a Pastor leaves a church, that is a very good time for the church to review its **Official Procedures and Policies** related to considering and calling a Pastoral Candidate. It is also a good idea to review them again, after calling a new Pastor.

## The Following are Specific Policies to Consider:

### 2.1. Policies for Accepting Names to Consider.

You need to determine a policy for accepting names to consider as Candidates. Many names will often be submitted which do not quality.

### Two Very Important Polices:

○ Anyone who submits their own name shall not be considered (Proverbs 27:2).

○ A written recommendation must be submitted for any Prospective Candidate.

### 2.2. The Candidating Procedure.

You need a specific step-by-step procedure to determine how a Prospective Candidate becomes a Candidate and then what steps to follow to determine if you should call the Candidate as Pastor.

If this is not spelled out specifically in your **Constitution and By-laws** you need to put together a Proposed Procedure and submit it to the Church for review and approval. This book addresses Recommended Procedures for Calling a Pastor.

### 2.3. The Procedure for Calling a Pastor.

You need a policy stating how to conduct a vote on calling a Candidate as a Pastor. You also need an official policy on how to negotiate the details of that call. There are times a Candidate will get the necessary votes for a call but is unable to accept that call.

After you extend the call to someone and negotiate the details, you must set a date when he officially becomes your Pastor. It is fitting and proper to have a **Pastoral Installation Service** where he officially becomes Pastor. Churches often host a dinner or refreshments after that service. You should invite the Pastors you used as your counselors and advisors during the candidating procedure to participate in the service. It is common to hold this service on a Saturday or Sunday afternoon or evening so others can attend.

## 2.4.  Financial Compensation.

**Three Areas of Financial Compensation to Address:**

○  **Funding the Activities of the Pastoral Search Committee.**

○  **Financially Compensating Those Who Fill the Pulpit as Guest Speakers or Candidates.**

These materials contain suggested guidelines for a compensation policy.

○  **A Basic Compensation Package.**

Present this to Prospective Candidates.

## A Basic Compensation Package Should Address the Following:

-  Salary and the Procedure for Review & Raises
-  Retirement
-  Housing Allowance or Equity Position *(if you have a Parsonage).*
-  Phone Allowance
-  Car Allowance
-  Medical Insurance
-  Day School Tuition *(if children)*
-  Continuing Education Allowance & Policy
-  Conference Expenses
-  Book Allowance
-  Missions Trips
-  Vacations
-  Sabbatical Policy
-  Moving Expenses
-  Compensation for the Pastor's Wife

## 3. Review Your Severance & Termination Policies.

You need to have Severance and Termination policies in place. This is a very important topic often not addressed. Too often these end up being more ideal and philosophical than practical.

After a Pastor leaves a church, it is a good idea to review the Severance and Termination policies.

These materials address the Severance and Termination polices in more detail in a later section.

## 4. Determine Policies for Contacting Candidates Currently Serving Another Church.

When a Pastoral Search Committee looks for a Candidate, they often look for unemployed Pastors or those they learn are looking for a church. Those are not the only source. Sometimes they are not the best source.

The best thing for a church to do is to determine first *what you are looking for in a Pastor*. After you determine what you *want* in a Pastor, seek recommendations from those you respect and trust. Ask for help finding contacts for that type of person. Those recommendations may lead you to an unemployed Pastor, but many times, they may lead you to one of the best sources for a Candidate, men currently serving in a church.

There are Pastors currently Pastoring a church, whom God wants to move on. Sometimes God has made that clear to them, other times, they have not discovered that. More often than not, it is like Paul and the Macedonian Vision (Acts 16:6-10). They are faithfully serving and heading in the direction God led them until one day He makes it clear they are to go somewhere else.

The ministry of being a Pastor is one of the Occupational Ministries, God lists in Ephesians 4:11. Pastors are a ministry God gives to *the churches*. Notice the plural word *churches*. Pastors are not for only one church. Sometimes God may have a person serve as a Pastor in one church for many years. Other times, God has them serve in one church for only a few years and then has them go to another church.

## O    Important Warning:

If you consider contacting a man, serving in another church, you must realize you need to deal with them a little differently, than you would with one who is not serving as a Pastor.

In many cases, those currently serving may not be considering a move. In most cases, if it becomes known they are consider candidating, it can cause problems in their current ministry.

It is not wise for a Pastor to announce to their church, they are looking for another church unless they are sure God clearly told them to move on. If they make such an announcement that will usually hinder their ministry. They should privately go through the initial Prospective Candidating step, and wait until they receive an invitation to be an actual Candidate, before they announce, to their church they are considering leaving their current ministry. The Church, which contacted them about being a Prospective Candidate, may decide not to call them as a Candidate, so the Prospective Candidate may never become an actual Candidate.

Consider this; how you would feel if your spouse told you, he or she was considering leaving you? It would hurt deeply. You would feel betrayed. Even if nothing happened, your relationship would be in serious trouble.

I know Pastors whom another church contacted to ask if they would consider being a Prospective Candidate. They mentioned the invitation to their current church. That caused people in their church to question that Pastor's commitment to their current ministry. That also caused some of those churches to ask themselves why their Pastor would consider leaving.

There were two types of responses from those churches. Some of those churches examined themselves, made changes and tried to persuade their Pastor to stay. In other cases, the Pastor's willingness to consider an invitation to candidate for another church caused them to feel betrayed. They lost confidence in their Pastor and asked him to resign. The sad thing is, in each case, there was not an actual invitation for a Pastor to leave their current church, just an invitation to become a Prospective Candidate

Sometimes it can be good for a Pastor to experience being contacted and to go quietly through the initial Prospective Candidating Procedure for God to assure them He wants them to stay in their current ministry or to prepare them for moving on.

If a Pastor takes that first step and accepts the invitation to be a Prospective Candidate, and the Church asks them to take the next step, and they believe God also wants them to take the next step, at that time, they need to inform their current ministry of that decision.

I know some Pastors whom other churches asked to consider being a Candidate and they did not mention the invitation to their church. They took the first step but either they or the church inviting them decided not to go any further. That was a wake-up call for those Pastors. God used that to help them recommit themselves to their current church. God blessed both them and their church.

## ○ How to Proceed:

When considering a Pastor who is currently serving in a church, a couple of members of the Pastoral Search Committee should go casually to that Pastor's church to hear him speak. It is best not to sit together. After hearing the Pastor speak, follow the normal candidating procedure.

It is inappropriate to contact leaders in the Pastor's current church, before he is an Official Candidate, unless he grants specific permission. It is best not to contact those people until your church and he agree to continue with the candidating procedure. That then becomes the time to request references from the leadership of his current church.

# Step 6.
# Review the Biblical Qualifications for a Pastor.

Three words are used in the Bible for Pastors, they are **Pastor, Elder** and **Bishop**. Books have been written examining and expounding on the meaning of these three words. Here is a brief look at each of them:

- **Pastor**
  (Ephesians 4:11)

  Pastor is one of the five Occupational Ministries God gives to the churches. There are various types of Pastoral Ministries, only one is being a Pastor.

  The word *Pastor* refers to the work of a *Shepherd,* particularly the work of *pasturing* the sheep. The focus of Pastoral ministry is to make sure the sheep are watched over and properly feed. The person in a Pastoral Ministry does the same as a Shepherd does with sheep, he feeds the sheep by bringing them to where the food is (John 21:16-17; 1 Peter 5:2; Psalm 23).

- **Elder** (1 Peter 5:1)

  The word *Elder* is the translation of the Greek word **presbuteros.** Elder identifies the *person,* who is a spiritual leader in the church. One of those elders is a Pastor.

- **Bishop** (1 Timothy 3:1; Titus 1:7)

  The word *Bishop* is the translation of the Greek word, **episcope.** Bishop focuses on the *work* of a specific Elder who is the Pastor, the spiritual leader in the church.

Notice the distinction between the words. *Elder* refers to the *person* and *Bishop* refers the *work*. The word Bishop is never used in a hierarchal sense in the Bible, though some groups use it to indicate one Pastor over other Pastors.

There are very specific qualifications in the Bible, which a Pastor **must** meet. They are not optional. It is very important to look at each qualification and determine what it means. Good churches differ over this. Your church must determine specifically what they mean to you.

## 1.    Qualifications Listed in 1 Timothy 3:1-7.

The Bible says it is a good thing to desire this work (v.1). Then it lists very specific required qualifications.

> This is a true saying, If a man desire the office of a bishop, he desireth a good work. A bishop then **must be** blameless, the husband of one wife, vigilant, sober, of good behaviour, given to hospitality, apt to teach; Not given to wine, no striker, not greedy of filthy lucre; but patient, not a brawler, not covetous; One that ruleth well his own house, having his children in subjection with all gravity; (For if a man know not how to rule his own house, how shall he take care of the church of God?) Not a novice, lest being lifted up with pride he fall into the condemnation of the devil. Moreover he must have a good report of them which are without; lest he fall into reproach and the snare of the devil.
>
> 1 Timothy 3:1-7

Look at each of the qualifications from that passage:

○    **Blameless** (v. 2)

The Greek word used here, ***anipilepton***, does not mean perfect; otherwise there would be no Pastors. This word means *one who does not have anything negative, which his adversaries can charge him.*

○    **The Husband of One Wife** (v. 2)

Many agree this means a Pastor may not be a woman, because a woman cannot be the husband.

Many interpret this to mean a Pastor *must* be a married man. This is reaffirmed later in verse 4, where it speaks of his children. That makes it seem there is a Biblical prohibition against a single man serving as a Pastor.

What about the phrase, *husband of one wife*? In Greek it says *mias gunaikos andra*, which literally says, *one woman man*. Does this mean the Pastor may only have one wife at a time *(as opposed to polygamy)*, or does it mean he may only have one wife ever *(meaning no divorce or remarriage under any circumstance, even the death of a spouse)*? Some scholars take it to mean both. What is your church's position?

○ **Vigilant** (v. 2)

This word, *nephaleon*, literally means, *to abstain from wine*, but it came to mean *a focused individual who does not get sidetracked.*

○ **Sober** (v. 2)

A modern interpretation of this verse would be one who does not get drunk but stays sober. Though that may be a correct application, this Greek word, *sophrona*, literally means *clear minded.*

○ **Of Good Behavior** (v. 2)

The Greek word here, *kosmion*, means *one whose has a good lifestyle*. This is a very simple one and easy to check out.

○ **Given to Hospitality** (v. 2)

This is the translation of the compound Greek word, *philoxenos*. The first part of the word, *philo* means *showing brotherly love*. The last part of the word, *xenos*, means *strangers*.

This came to mean *one who makes people feel welcome and opens his heart and home to them, especially to strangers.*

If someone is a good preacher but is not hospitable, they need a different ministry. If they do not meet this qualification, they may not be Pastors.

○ **Apt to Teach** (v. 2)

The Greek word used here is **didaktikon** which means *one who can teach*. Notice it does not say they must have the *Gift of Teaching*. The word used in this passage literally means they need to be *the kind of person who can teach others*. That is different from the *Gift of Teaching*.

○ **Not Given to Wine** (v. 3)

This is two Greek words, **me paroinon**. When the Greek word **me**, appears before another word, it is similar to saying *Never*. The second word here **paroinon**, means *next to wine*. This literally means *one who is **never** next to wine*.

If they are never *next to wine (the most common alcoholic beverage in biblical times)*, then then will never be drinking wine. Many believe this means a Pastor must be one who does not drink alcoholic beverages.

○ **No Striker** (v. 3)

This Greek word, **plekten**, refers to physically striking someone else. Here it means *someone who does not physically fight with others*.

○ **Not Greedy of Filthy Lucre** (v. 3)

This is the translation of the Greek words, **me aischrokerdes**. It means *someone who is **never** willing to do wrong or bend the rules so they can profit*.

Too many people believe in *situational ethics*, where the ends justify the means, or they are willing to bend the rules, depending on the situation, even in ministry. People like that do not meet this qualification.

We need people who embrace what Dr. Bob Jones, Sr., a faithful preacher for many decades, said, *It is never right to do wrong, to do right.*

○ **Patient** (v. 3)

The Greek word used here, ***epieike***, means *one who waits to make sure things are dealt with fairly*, as opposed to being impetuous.

○ **Not a Brawler** (v. 3)

The Greek word here is ***amachos***. The word ***macho***, means *one who fights contentiously with words*. The ***a*** in front of a word means *a very strong not*. ***Amachos***, means *one who **absolutely does not** fight contentiously with words.*

○ **Not Covetous** (v. 3)

The Greek words used here, ***me aphilarguros***, mean *he is **not** be a person who is **ever** consumed with the desire for personal, material or financial gain*. This disqualifies many from ministry.

○ **One Who Rules Well His Own House** (v. 4-5)

How does he handle his family? This verse does not say, ***IF** he has a family he must rule it well*. It says, *one who rules well his own house.* It then goes on and mentions his children.

To rule your own house and have children indicates you are married and have children. That means these verses indicate he must be a married man, with children and he must have his family in order.

These verses go on and state if a man does not know how to raise his family, he will not know how to Pastor a church. Therefore, if you accept these verses for what they say, these verses seem to preclude an unmarried man or a married man without any children from being a Pastor.

This also makes it clear those who live under his roof *(his own house)* must follow his leadership.

Some interpret this to mean there is no room in the Pastorate for any man whose children, at any time in their life, regardless of their age, do not walk with the Lord. These verses do not say *his children must walk with the Lord.* No one can make their children accept Christ, or live for the Lord. It says he *must rule them well* and they must be in *subjection.* In other words, they must listen to and follow his rules. If a man's children do not listen to him and follow his rules, then he cannot be a Pastor. It is important to understand; children can listen to rules and follow them but not have faith in Christ.

Does this rule apply to those children who have grown and left the home? Some say yes, some say no.

○ **Not a Novice** (v. 6)

These words *me neophuton,* mean *he must not be unexperienced.* A Pastor must have a record of accomplishment in Christian service.

Pride is problem with many young preachers. This verse says they need to serve under someone first to learn servitude; otherwise Satan can defeat them with pride.

A church, which calls a Pastor right out of Seminary, who has not served in some type of ministry internship, is making a big mistake.

## 2. Qualifications Listed in Titus 1:5-9.

Some of the qualifications mentioned, in the other passages are repeated here, others are added. See the above for explanations of the repeated qualifications.

Some scholars believe these qualifications are not just for Pastors but should apply to any spiritual leader *(using the broader definition of the word elder used in this verse)* in the church. Notice the word, **must** is used again. These qualifications are not optional.

For this cause left I thee in Crete, that thou shouldest set in order the things that are wanting, and ordain elders in every city, as I had appointed thee: If any be blameless, the husband of one wife, having faithful children not accused of riot or unruly. For a bishop **must** be blameless, as the steward of God; not selfwilled, not soon angry, not given to wine, no striker, not given to filthy lucre; But a lover of hospitality, a lover of good men, sober, just, holy, temperate; Holding fast the faithful word as he hath been taught, that he may be able by sound doctrine both to exhort and to convince the gainsayers.                                   Titus 1:5-9

O    **Blameless** (v. 6)

See previous passage.

O    **Husband of One Wife** (v. 6)

See previous passage.

O    **Having Faithful Children Not Accused of Riot or Unruly** (v. 6)

Notice the focus is not on the children's *faith* but on their *actions*.

O    **Blameless, as the Steward of God** (v.7)

This is the same word *blameless*, used in verse six, but here the words, as the steward of God are added. That means *he must have his finances in order*.

O    **Not Self-Willed** (v. 7)

The Greek words used here *me authade*, mean *one who never puts their own pleasure (will) first*. Determine if he puts himself or others first.

O    **Not Soon Angry** (v. 7)

The Greek words used here are *me orgilos*. There are a number of different words in Greek for *anger*. The Bible teaches there is a time when anger is okay (Ephesians 4:26). *Orgilos*, the word used for *anger* in this verse means *one who is prone to getting angry.* The King James Version translates this very well when it uses the words, *not soon angry.* There is a place for anger but if someone easily gets angry, then they should not be a Pastor.

○  **Not Given to Wine** (v. 7)

See previous passage.

○  **No Striker** (v. 7)

See previous passage.

○  **Not Given to Filthy Lucre** (v. 7)

The same as *Not Covetous,* in the previous passage.

○  **Lover of Hospitality** (v. 8)

See previous passage.

○  **Lover of Good Men** (v. 8)

This translates one Greek word, ***philagathon.*** It means *a liker of good men.* He needs to *like* people. It is harder to *like* someone than to love them.

○  **Sober** (v. 8)

See previous passage.

○  **Just** (v. 8)

This word ***dikaion*** means *one who follows God's laws.* He must follow what is just and right in God's eyes, applying the Biblical principles to his life.

○  **Holy** (v. 8)

This is not ***agios***, the usual Greek word for holy, which means *set apart unto God.* This is the Greek word ***osios***. It means *to be set apart from things considered morally wrong by the society where one lives.*

This means, if a Pastor were in an area where they consider certain behavior offensive, like what you eat or wear, he would be careful about those things.

A Pastor should seek to be culturally sensitive. For example, working in a predominately-Jewish or Muslim community he would not eat pork.

O   **Temperate** (v. 8)

This Greek word, ***egkrate***, means *one who has mastery over himself.* He needs to live a disciplined *(tempered)* life.

O   **Holding Fast the Faithful Word as He Hath Been Taught** (v. 9)

He needs to study the Word of God, learn from other Bible teachers and stand firm on his doctrine.

O   **Be Able By Sound Doctrine to Exhort & Convince the Gainsayers** (v. 9)

He has to know how to use the Word of God to deal with people who normally refuse to listen *(the gainsayers)*.

## 3.   Qualifications Listed in 1 Peter 5:1-4.

The elders which are among you I exhort, who am also an elder, and a witness of the sufferings of Christ, and also a partaker of the glory that shall be revealed: Feed the flock of God which is among you, taking the oversight thereof, not by constraint, but willingly; not for filthy lucre, but of a ready mind; Neither as being lords over God's heritage, but being ensamples to the flock. And when the chief Shepherd shall appear, ye shall receive a crown of glory that fadeth not away.

1 Peter 5:1-4

O   **Feed the Flock of God**

Middle Eastern Shepherds did not give food to the sheep; they brought the sheep to where the food was. A Pastor is a Spiritual Shepherd who makes sure believers get spiritual nutrition through the preaching, teaching and instruction in personal study of the Word of God.

○ **Taking the Oversight**

They keep a watchful eye on the sheep, providing leadership and protection, not because no one else will do it, and not because of the financial benefits.

## 4. Personal & Professional Qualifications.

The Personal and Professional Qualifications for a Pastor are addressed in the section on *Determining the Qualifications for a Pastor*.

# Identify Your Church's Position On Principles & Practices

The purpose of the Pastoral Search Committee is to act on behalf of the church in screening, contacting and interviewing possible Candidates for the position of Pastor. In order to do that it needs to understand the church's *Positions* on various issues, before it invites someone to be a Candidate. It is not the responsibility of the Pastoral Search Committee to determine those *Positions*, but to be sure they are identified, and if necessary, clarify them.

There are some Principles and Practices, I recommend you identify if you have a specific position on, even if it may not seem important to some people in your church. You must understand all the items addressed in this section are important to some Pastors.

Many times a denominational name gives people an idea of a basic doctrinal set of beliefs. One of the weaknesses of a church calling itself a *Bible Church* or *Community Church* is there is nothing in the name to indicate its beliefs. A Bible Church could be Calvinistic or Arminian, Pre-millennial or Amillennial, Charismatic or Non-Charismatic. That is why some Bible and Community Churches have a smaller identifier phrase along with their name such as, *A Reformed Church* or *A Baptist Church*. That helps people get some idea of their doctrinal beliefs.

You need to identify where you, as a church, currently stand on these issues and on various ministries, even if your position is *no preference*. If an item is not important to you, make a statement you do not have a specific position. Keep in mind, some of these items, which may not seem important to you, are very important to some Candidates you may consider.

I knew a church that had no idea a position on music or dress standards was important to some Pastors, so they never addressed that issue. The Pastor they called felt those were *priority items* but did not address those issues with that church before they called him. He believed it was morally wrong for singers to sing using sound tracks *(pre-recorded music)*. He also believed it was immoral for women to wear slacks. *[Deuteronomy 22:5 is one of the proof texts for that belief].* Having no idea anyone held to those beliefs, that church called him as Pastor.

The first night that new Pastor was in the church a women wearing slacks sang special music with a sound track. He felt he could not let that pass. He publically expressed his opinion very strongly. People were shocked. In less than two weeks, they were looking for a new Pastor again.

I must repeat this, each one of the following positions or practices are important to *some* Pastors. Many Pastors may not have experience or background in all these areas, but most have some sort of opinion. It is important to identify if your Church has a position on each of the following. It is likely you will not have position on some of these items. Once you determine your opinion, do not provide this information to a Candidate until they have completed the *Pastoral Candidate Questionnaire.* That will help you get a better idea where they stand.

## 1.    Doctrine.

You must clearly identify your church's Official Doctrinal Positions. Doctrine is the set of beliefs held by a church or individual. It is very important to identify what doctrine your church believes. Every church should have a **Doctrinal Statement**, clearly set forth, in its **Constitution**. Some Doctrinal Statements are very brief some are very specific.

Does your Church's Doctrinal Statement truly reflect what your church believes? A church should hold true to its founding Doctrinal Statement but many churches have not reviewed their Doctrinal Statement in years and most people in the church no longer believe some of the items contained therein. Most people do not realize a Church's Constitution is a *legally binding document.* Most Church Constitutions contain a Doctrinal Statement. If yours does, then members are legally, morally and ethically bound to agree with its Doctrinal Statement or forgo the right to vote or hold office.

When people join a church, most Church Constitutions require they agree with the church's Doctrinal Statement. If the beliefs of any people in your church are not in agreement with that Doctrinal Statement, those people may not vote, no matter what percentage of the church they represent. That can create a problem, especially for a church who neglected to inform people of its Doctrinal Statement or which allowed people to join who do not agree with the Church's Doctrinal Statement.

This is not an arbitrary matter, nor one that is simple to correct. Even if the overwhelming majority in a church no longer agrees with the Church's Doctrinal Statement, acknowledgment that a person does not agree with the Doctrinal Statement legally disqualifies them from voting. That means the majority cannot vote to change the Constitution, because they cannot legally vote.

If a church realizes many people no longer adhere to some points in its Doctrinal Statement and want to change or remove those items, here is a moral, ethical, legal and peaceful way to resolve the problem. Those who do not agree with the Church's Doctrinal Statement, should identify how they differ with the Church's Doctrinal Statement and recommend the Church consider making specific changes. Those should then either resign *(as legally obligated by the Church Constitution),* or abstain from voting on the recommendations for change. Those who still agree with the Doctrinal Statement should then decide if they are willing to have the church make the recommended changes. This does not mean they change what they as individuals believe, it just means they are willing to let the Church change what people need to acknowledge they believe in order to belong to the church as Voting Members. Unless a church undertakes some steps like this, a small minority, has legal grounds to expel those who do not agree with the Church's Doctrinal Statement.

I know a church, which was making some changes to improve the effectiveness of their ministry. A very small minority opposed the changes. That minority discovered the people wanting to make the changes did not believe some items in the Church's Doctrinal Statement. Rather than negotiating and discussing items, the majority assumed they could resolve the matter by following the amendment procedure in the Church Constitution. They decided to make an amendment to the Constitution and change the Doctrinal Statement. The minority pointed out the Constitution said a member had to agree with the Doctrinal Statement.

The majority consulted an attorney and discovered they did not have any legal standing. If the majority had ignored the minority and passed the amendment, and then the minority challenged them in court, the majority would have lost. In that case, the majority happened to be the nicer group, but they realized they could no longer be members of that church. They left and started another church.

Make sure you know what your church believes about the following doctrinal items. If your **Church Doctrinal Statement** does not address some of these items, try to get a consensus of what your church believes.

Doctrinal positions are important to most people in ministry. The following are some doctrinal issues you should be sure to clarify:

○ **Bibliology – The Doctrine of the Bible**

Many churches have very different views about the inspiration and authority of scripture

- Some churches state they believe the Bible is the inspired word of God. That can mean different things.

Some state they believe the Bible is the *inspired, infallible,* and *inerrant* Word of God?

What is your church's position on inspiration?

Have a Prospective Candidate define what they believe in relation to these three "I"s: Inspiration, Infallibility and Inerrancy.

- Do you believe in the *Grammatical Historical* interpretation of the Bible, often referred to as *literal interpretation?* That means you believe **the words** in the Bible are inspired and should be interpreted literally according to the rules of grammar and in the way they would have been understood by the people first reading those words. Or does you church follow another view, such as the *Dynamic View* held by the translators of the *New International Version of the Bible*? That view says **the concepts, not the words**, are inspired.

- Do you believe God created the heavens, earth and everything else, in seven literal, 24-hour days as it says in Genesis?

- Do you believe the flood spoken of in Genesis was a literal world-wide flood?

- Do you believe a particular translation of the Bible is more reliable than others?
  Are there versions you do not want used?

O **Eschatology – The Second Coming**

There is a lot of division among Christian Churches on *Eschatology*, the doctrine regarding last days and the return of Christ. Most denominations have clearly defined eschatological positions. Ministers and many churches have a position on this.

Most denominations are *amillennial*. That means they do not believe in the Rapture of the Church or the Millennial Rule of Christ. They believe most events in the Book of Revelation were symbolic.

That following denominations hold to an official *amillennial position*: Roman Catholic, Greek Orthodox, Anglican, Lutheran, Reformed, New Covenant and Presbyterian. Some individual ministers and congregations in those denominations may have different views but *amillennialism* is the official doctrine of those denominations.

45

Some denominations and churches such as most Baptists, Assemblies of God and Brethren are ***pre-millennial.*** They believe Christ will return for His church literally and physically, before He reigns for 1,000 years on earth in a literal fulfillment of God's promises to Israel.

There are three major different schools of thought among ***pre-millennials***. Some pre-millennials hold to a ***Pre-Tribulation*** return of Christ, where all believers will be raptured before the tribulation. Some hold to a ***Mid-Tribulation*** return, where Christ removes all believers halfway through the Tribulation. Some hold to a ***Post-Tribulation*** return of Christ, where Christ returns after the Tribulation and immediately before the Judgment and Christ's millennial rule on earth.

Some churches, like the United Methodist Church do not have an official position on eschatology.

What a person believes about the return of Christ is important. It effects how they view the world and does have an effect on how they minister.

- What is your position regarding the return of Christ?
  Is it *premillennial, postmillennial* or *amillennial*?

- Do you believe in the Rapture of the Church?
  If so, do you hold to a *pre-millennial, pre-tribulation rapture* or some other position?

## ○ <u>Soteriology</u> – The Doctrine of Salvation

Here is a very controversial area. Some churches are *Calvinistic*, some are *Arminian*, some are somewhere in-between and some have no position. Most ministers have a very clear position on this.

Those who are *Calvinistic* believe the term *election* means God predetermined who will be saved and who will not. Those who follow the *Arminian* teaching believe anyone can be saved.

Does your church believe in *Eternal Security* or the Calvinistic doctrine, *Perseverance of the Saints?* These are quite different.

*Eternal Security* teaches once a person is born again, they are always saved, regardless of their subsequent lifestyle. That teaching is contrary to *Arminianism,* which believes a person can lose their salvation. On the other hand, *Calvinism* teaches *Perseverance of the Saints,* which teaches those who are saved will continue to live a godly lifestyle. According to that teaching, if a person's subsequent lifestyle reflects continued ungodliness, they were never saved. The *Arminian teaching* says if a person's subsequent lifestyle stops reflecting godliness, that person lost their salvation. The *Calvinist* does not teach they lost it, they teach that person never had it. Both view the person as unsaved. The person who holds to *Eternal Security* sees the person as saved but backslidden.

It is very important to ask a Candidate to clarify their position on this issue.

- Who can be saved?

- How does a person receive salvation?

- Is your church *Calvinistic, Arminian* or something else? How important is this to you?

## O <u>Pneumatology</u> – The Doctrine of the Holy Spirit

What people believe about the Holy Spirit is another very controversial area. There is one area where there is great division, even though God says there must be understanding and agreement (1 Corinthians 12:1-6).

I recommend reading my book, *Unraveling the Holy Spirit Controversy.*

- When do you believe a person receives the Holy Spirit?

- List the Gifts of the Holy Spirit and a brief explanation of each.

- What is your position on the *Pentecostal* and *Charismatic* movements?

- What is your position on the Baptism of the Holy Spirit?

- What is your position on Tongues?

- What is your position on Healing?

- What is your position on Laying on Hands and Anointing with Oil?

○ **Ecclesiology – The Doctrine of the Church**

What is your position on Ecclesiology, the doctrine of the Church? Some churches teach they are the only true church. Some teach all true believers in Christ are mystically part of a *Universal, Invisible Church*. Others refer to the union all believers have as *the Family of God*, and believe the term *Church* refers to *Local Assemblies* of believers.

The other important practical distinction, which must be understood, is a how is a church to be administered? For some this is philosophy, for others it is part of the doctrine of the church.

Some churches are *denominational*, with a hierarchal structure, which oversees individual churches. That includes denominations such as the Roman Catholic Church, the Anglican Church, Presbyterian Church, United Methodist Church, American Baptists and others. Denominations often own the buildings and help provide Pastors.

Some churches are autonomous, with each local church being self-governing and not accountable to a higher body. It is incorrect to refer to them as a denomination. That includes Southern Baptists, Independent Baptists, Assemblies of God and most Bible Churches. Some autonomous churches may appear to others to be a denomination, when they work together with other churches and form associations or conventions such as the *Baptist Bible Fellowship, Southern Baptist Convention* or *Independent Fundamental Churches of America.* They are still all independent churches.

How is your church administered? The Presbyterian Church and many Bible Churches believe a Board of Elders should run the church. Many Baptist churches believe a church should be led by a Pastor, with Deacons and other officers assisting in some areas, and the congregation having the final say. Some churches believe a church should be run by a Church Board. Some believe a church should be run by the congregation.

Most Pastors and many churches have very strong positions on these issues.

- Do you believe in a distinction between the *Family of God* and the *Local Church*?

- Who is responsible for the administration of the church?
  Is your church a Pastor led, Elder led, Board led or Congregation led church?

- What are the Official Officers in your church?

- What is the role of the Pastor?

- What decisions can the Pastor make without approval from the board or church?

- What decisions does the Pastor need approval from the board or church?

- How do you view the church's role in World Evangelism?

## 2. Personal Standards.

Personal Standards include a variety of very personal issues. Some of these personal standards may not be important to some people, yet some are very important to others.

Some Pastors have personal preferences regarding some of these. Others feel so strongly about their personal standards they refer to them as *convictions* and are willing to fight for them. It is important to know if you, or any Prospective Candidate, have a position on any of the following:

- ○ Men's & Women's Clothing
- ○ Tattoos
- ○ Hair Length & Styles
- ○ Piercing
- ○ Use of Tobacco
- ○ Use of Alcohol
- ○ Music
- ○ Card Playing
- ○ Gambling and the Lottery
- ○ Attending Movie Theatres
- ○ Cable & Satellite TV, Renting Videos
- ○ Attending Plays & Broadway Productions
- ○ Dancing
- ○ Mixed Bathing *(both sexes swimming together)*
- ○ Dating – who should date, chaperones, etc.
- ○ Interracial or Cross Cultural Dating or Marriage

## 3. Philosophy of Ministry.

You need a written *Philosophy of Ministry.* This is composed of a Purpose Statement and an explanation of *why you do what you do.*

Every Pastor has a *Philosophy of Ministry*, which guides them in most decisions they make. It is important you determine what your church's *Philosophy of Ministry* is, so you can find a Pastor who is truly compatible with you.

- ○ **What is the Purpose of Your Church?**

    A written *Purpose Statement* for your church is usually in your **Church Constitution**.

50

O   **Why Do You Do What You Do?**

This is an incredibly important question to ask. Most churches do things a certain way because that is the way they did them for a long time. Sometimes they do not know *why* they do things a certain way.

*Doctrine* and the *Purpose* for the Church should never change, but some *methods* should change. Look at every aspect of your church's program and ask why you do things the way you do.

Be careful about making changes before you call a new Pastor. If you feel, you need to make changes, choose a Pastor you feel will help guide you into those changes.

## 4.   Worship & Pulpit Ministry.

The Worship and Pulpit Ministry are a very significant part of Pastoral Ministry. All Pastors, and some people in your church, will have very strong beliefs about this area of ministry. Some are very flexible about certain elements of the worship and pulpit ministry, some are not flexible at all.

For most of church history, most churches only met once a week on a Sunday Morning. In the 1950's through the 1990's things changed. Many churches started to hold services Sunday Morning and Sunday Evening. Some held another during the middle of the week, often called Mid-Week Service or Prayer Meeting. Back then, the Sunday Morning Service was held almost universally at 11 a.m. Many churches held their Mid-Week Meeting on Wednesdays.

During the 1990's many churches began to make changes. Some attribute it to the *Small Group Movement* others attribute it to other changes in society. Service times changed. Many churches began to hold their Sunday Morning Service earlier.

Many churches began to eliminate their Sunday Evening Service and then the Mid-Week Service.

New churches starting in the 1990's, and later, often only held Sunday Morning Services. Some of them grew significantly. They have active ministries but still do not hold Sunday Evening nor Mid-Week Services.

Churches need to look carefully at what services they conduct and why. They need to realize many Churches and Pastors no longer view Sunday Evening or Mid-Week Services as part of a regular church ministry.

In many churches, Music is a very important part of the Worship Ministry. The next item, after this one, addresses the Music Ministry separately.

- What are the days and times of your regular services?
  Why do you meet at those times?
- What does each service generally consist of?
  Why?
- Who determines the format and content of your worship services?
- Do you use drama in any services?
- Who determines who speaks in the pulpit, such as: Evangelists, Teachers or Guest Speakers?
- Do you use a church bulletin?
  If so, who prepares it?
  Does it contain an order of service?
- Do you use projection in your church?
- Do you use a sound system?
  Do you have wireless microphones?
- Do you have headsets for the hearing impaired?
- Are your services broadcast, either on radio or television?
- How do you conduct Invitations in your church?
  How often?
- Who counsels those who respond to an Invitation?

❍ Do you have Ushers?
How are they chosen?
How long do they serve?
What do they do?

## 5. Music.

Music is usually an important part of most worship services. In some churches, music it is a very significant part of ministry.

Some churches have Song Leaders, Worship Leaders, Music Directors or Worship Teams, who play a significant role in the Worship Ministry. Some of those people see their role as assisting the Pastor in the Worship Ministry. On the other hand, some see the Pastor's role strictly as a Pulpit Ministry, and believe he should not have a leading role, making decisions about the other aspects of the Worship Ministry. Some Pastors have experience in both of those settings.

You need to determine if the people involved in your Music Ministry, as well as the Prospective Candidate have the same viewpoints about this area of ministry. Determine if they are willing to make changes.

❍ Is there right and wrong music for Christians?

❍ What type of music do you use in your church?

❍ Do you ever use pre-recorded accompaniment music *(sound tracks)* in your church?

❍ What instruments do you use in your church?

❍ Are there certain instruments you do not want used in your church?

❍ Who determines what music is used in your church?

❍ Who should select the songs for the services?

❍ Who should lead songs in the service?

❍ Do you do special musical programs such as cantatas or musicals?
If so, who chooses them?

Who directs those?

O    Do you have a choir, ensemble or praise team?

O    What are the requirements to sing special music in your church?

O    Who determines who sings or plays special music in your church?

O    Who determines the specific songs to be sung or played for special music?

O    Do you have special concerts or traveling musicians come minister in your church?
Who are some of the artists you previously scheduled?

O    Who determines if you have concerts, who comes and when they are held?

## 6.    Sunday School.

When you look at Church History, you will discover Sunday School is a relatively new ministry. Robert Raikes started the Sunday School Movement and held the first Sunday Schools in England in 1780's.

For the next 170 years, Sunday School remained a ministry mainly for children. By the mid-1950's, Sunday School grew and became a major ministry in many churches. They offered classes for everyone including children and adults. Those were held before or after the Regular Worship Service. That boom lasted about 50 years.

In the 1990's, church's began to change their Worship Services, and Sunday School became to decline. Over the past few decades, many smaller churches eliminated Adult Sunday School. Some began to run their Sunday School for Children at the same time as their Morning Worship Service. Then some medium and larger churches eliminated Sunday School.

O    Do you have a Sunday School?

❍ Who oversees the Sunday School?

❍ What classes do you offer?
Do you have classes for specific ages?

❍ When and where do your classes meet?

❍ What curriculum do you use?

❍ Who are your Sunday School Teachers?
How do you choose them?

❍ What are the Qualifications and Standards of Conduct for teachers?

❍ Do you do a background check on all Sunday School workers who work with children and teens, as recommended by all church insurance companies and by many state laws?

❍ What are the responsibilities of your Sunday School Teachers and Workers?

❍ What is the length of a Sunday School Teachers term?

❍ Do you have *Teachers in Training* working with each teacher?

❍ How do you evaluate your teachers?

❍ If a teacher is unable to attend one week, what happens to their class?

❍ What training do you provide Sunday School teachers and workers?

## 7. Nursery, Toddlers & Beginners Ministry.

Many churches conduct a Nursery, Toddlers and Beginners Ministry during the Morning Service. Some churches, who offer Adult Sunday School Classes, offer a Nursery, Toddlers and Beginners Ministry during Sunday School. Some churches combine those groups. In many churches, they call this entire area of ministry the Nursery.

❍ Do you have a Nursery, Toddlers & Beginners Ministry?

○ During what services is it provided?

○ Who oversees the Nursery Ministry?

○ Who works in the Nursery? How do you select those workers?

○ What are the Qualifications and Standards of Conduct for Nursery workers?

○ Do you do a background check on all Nursery workers, as recommended by all church insurance companies and by many state laws?

○ What is the length of a Nursery workers term?

○ What materials do you use in your Nursery Ministry?

○ How do you deal with disciplinary problems in the Nursery?

## 8.    Children's Ministries (PreK-6th Grade).

During the 1950's many churches expanded their ministries to children to include additional ministries such as *Boy Scouts, Girl Scouts, Boys Brigade, Pioneer Girls, AWANA, Word of Life Clubs, Royal Rangers, Good News Clubs* and others. Many churches held these ministries on a weeknight. Some churches held these at the same time as the Sunday Evening or Mid-Week Service.

Some churches also held a Vacation Bible School (VBS), every summer for children. These usually lasted seven days, starting on a Monday and ending the following Sunday. Some churched conducted their VBS for two weeks.

Children's Ministries were strong for many years. Since the 1990's, things changed and there has been a serious decline in these ministries. Two-week Vacation Bible Schools changed to one week. Some changed to five days. Some eliminated them. Churches also began to eliminate many of the other Children's Ministries. Now some churches just hold special events or occasional community outreaches for children.

○ What specific ministries do you have to Children?

❍ Who works in these ministries?
How do you select them?

❍ What are the Qualifications and Standards of Conduct for Children's workers?

❍ Do you do a background check on all Children's workers, as recommend by all church insurance companies and by many state laws?

❍ What are your policies regarding Adults or Teens driving children to and from church?

❍ What is the length of a Children's workers term?

❍ What curriculum, program or materials do you use in your Children's Ministries?

❍ What facilities do they use and when do they meet?

❍ Do you have any children's choirs, singing groups or drama teams?

❍ Do you have any special fellowships or activities for children?

❍ Do you do any retreats or send your children to camp?
Are there specific camps you use or will not use?

❍ How do you deal with disciplinary problems in the Children's Ministry?

## 9. Youth Ministries (Teens, Gr. 7-12).

Youth Ministries is a generic term, which usually refers to ministries geared to Teens in grades 7-12. As with Children's Ministries, many of these started in the 1950's.

Many churches held what they called *Young People*'s meetings often on Sunday Evening, before, during or after the Evening Service.

Groups like *Youth for Christ, Word of Life* and *AWANA* developed materials and programs for these Youth Ministries. By the 1970's some churches were hiring Youth Pastors. Bible Colleges began to offer training for Youth Pastors.

Though many churches still have Youth Ministries, these too began to see a decline in the 1990's.

- ○ What specific ministries do you have to Teens?
- ○ Who works in these ministries?
- ○ What are the Qualifications and Standards of Conduct for Youth workers?
- ○ Do you do a background check on all Youth workers, as recommend by all church insurance companies and by many state laws?
- ○ How do you select Youth workers?
- ○ What is the length of a Youth workers term?
- ○ What are your policies regarding Adults or Teens driving others to and from church activities?
- ○ What curriculum, program or materials do you use in your Youth Ministries?
- ○ What facilities do they use and when do they meet?
- ○ Do you have any teen choirs, singing groups or drama teams?
- ○ Do you have any special fellowships or activities for teens?
- ○ Do you do service projects with your teens?
- ○ What opportunities for service are there in your church for teens?
- ○ Do you encourage your teens to go on short term missions trips?
  How do you encourage this?
  Who have they gone with?
  Where have they gone?
- ○ Do you do any retreats or do you send your teens to camp?
  Are there specific camps you use or will not use?
- ○ Do you provide career counseling for your teens?
- ○ How do you deal with disciplinary problems in the Youth Ministry?

## 10.    Specialized Ministries.

Some churches have a variety of other ministries, usually focused on a specific group of people.

O      Do you, or have you had, ministries to specific people such as:

- Senior Citizens
- Deaf
- Non-English Speakers, ESL/TESOL
- Singles
- Recovering Substance Abusers
- Nursing Homes
- Jails & Prisons
- Shut-Ins

O      How do you determine if a new ministry is started?

## 11.    Prayer Ministry.

From the 1950's through the 1990's many churches had what they called a Mid-Week Prayer Meeting. Some churches held a Sunday Evening Prayer Service and some had Morning Men's or Daytime Women's Prayer Groups. Some churches still have those ministries but many do not.

Some churches used weekly prayer lists to keep people informed of prayer needs in the church. Some had Prayer Chains to inform people by phone of urgent prayer needs. The prayer lists have survived in some churches, but social media replaced those and prayer chains in many churches.

O      What type of organized prayer ministries does your church have?
When and where do they meet?
Who participates in these?

O      Do you have a regularly updated prayer list whereby people may be informed of specific prayer needs? Who puts this together?

O      Do you have a prayer chain to inform people in your church of urgent prayer needs?

How is this set up?
Who coordinates this?

O    Do you have any regularly scheduled prayer times?

O    Do you observe the National Day of Prayer at your church?

## 12.    Fellowship.

Fellowship is an important part of a church. Years ago, many churches organized regular opportunities for fellowship, apart from the regular church services.

Some churches had regular committees to organize and implement these. Fellowships could include meals, activities, parties, projects and trips. Organized Church Fellowships have seen a decline in the past few decades.

O    What type of organized fellowships do you have?

O    Who coordinates the fellowships?

O    Do you as a church celebrate any of the following? How do you celebrate each one?
     Are there aspects to these celebrations in which a Christian should not partake?
     - Martin Luther King Day
     - Valentine's Day
     - President's Day
     - St. Patrick's Day
     - Easter
     - Mother's Day
     - Memorial Day
     - Father's Day
     - Independence Day
     - Labor Day
     - Clergy Appreciation Month
     - Columbus Day
     - Halloween
     - Veteran's Day
     - Thanksgiving
     - Christmas

- New Year's Eve
- Other Holidays or Special Days

O     Do you have regular, or periodic, church dinners?

O     Do you have a Men's Breakfast or Fellowship?
What is the purpose and format for this?
Who coordinates this?

O     Do you have a Ladies Luncheon or Fellowship?
What is the purpose and format for this?
Who coordinates this?

O     Do you do any out of church fellowship activities,
like trips or retreats together?

O     Do you have fun activities for your entire church
family?

O     Do you ever show films in your church?
If so when and what type?

## 13.    Visitors & Visitation.

During the 1950's through the 1970's, a time of great church growth, many churches had organized visitation programs. Those often included a follow-up portion for visiting members and attendees. Most were strongly evangelistic in nature.

Though some churches still have an organized Visitation Ministry, these began to see a decline in the 1980's and now very few churches have these.

Even though many churches do not have an organized visitation ministry, it is very important to make visitors feel welcome when they attend your church and to have some means of following up on them, as well as following up on members or attendees.

O     How do you keep track of visitors?

Do you use a Visitor's Card or Guest Book?

O    Do you use Greeters?
If so, how are these chosen?
What do they do?

O    How are Visitors followed up on?
Do they receive a letter or a visit?

O    Do you have an organized visitation program?
If so, how and when is it conducted?

## 14.    Outreach, Soul Winning, Evangelistic Meetings, Bus Ministry & Love in Action.

During the 1950's through the 1980's, many churches had very active Outreach, Soul-Winning and Bus Ministries.

A much older ministry and tradition, which lasted for almost two hundred years, was that of the Evangelistic or Revival Meeting. Those started in the 1700's and continued through the 1980's. Many churches had at least one annual Evangelistic or Revival Meeting. These began to see a decline in the 1990's.

After the turn of the century, some churches began to develop *Love in Action* type ministries as a way to express God's Love in practical ways to people in the community. These are community service ministries.

O    What evangelistic outreach do you have into your community?

O    Do you hold regular Evangelistic or Revival meetings?
If so, when?
Who are some speakers or groups you have had for these meetings

O    Do you have a specific Soul Winning Ministry?
If so, how is this run?

O    Do you have a Bus or Van Ministry?
If so, how is this run?

Do you have your own buses or vans or do you lease them?

O   Do you have gospel tracts available for your people? Who selects them?

O   Do you have a Welcome Wagon, or New Move type ministry?
If so, how is this run?

O   Do you have a presence at local community events, fairs, parades, etc.?

## 15.   Small Groups, Home Fellowships and Circles of Caring.

The 1980's began to see the *Home Bible Study and Small Group Movement*. These grew significantly in the 1990's and past the turn of the century. Most of these meet in homes.

In many churches, Small Groups began to replace Sunday Evening and Mid-Week Services and in some cases even the Sunday School. Jonathan Falwell, Pastor of *Thomas Road Baptist Church* in Lynchburg, Virginia, said their Sunday School classes are part of their small group ministry.

O   Do you have some type of small group ministry?

O   Who coordinates these ministries?

O   When and where do they meet?

O   What are the qualifications for someone to lead or host a small group?
Who determines these people?

O   How do you determine what is taught at your small group meetings?
Does your church use coordinated church-wide study materials for small groups?

O   How do you evaluate your small groups?

## 16.   Discipleship.

Discipleship is one of the main purposes for a church. Discipleship is the ministry of helping believers grow in Christ.

This is important for new believers as well as those who have been believers a long time.

The Worship and Pulpit Ministry, as well as the Sunday School, Bible Studies and Fellowships all play a role in discipleship.

Some churches have formalized individual and group discipleship programs, some do it with self-guided materials and some do it casually.

- How do you disciple people in your church?
- Do you have materials you use for new believers?
- What training do you provide to help your people have a daily personal time with God?
- How do you encourage your people to have family devotions?
- Do you encourage your families to use daily devotionals such as *The Daily Bread* or *Days of Praise?*

## 17. Counseling.

Every church has a responsibility to see its people receive Biblical Counseling when needed. It is interesting to note the Holy Spirit is called the *Comforter* (John 14:26). He can help get us through any situation. Often He uses people to help us do that.

The Bible says it is important where we get our counseling (Psalm 1:1). If the church does not provide counseling then where are people to go? Many people think they need to go to a psychologist or psychiatrist if they need counselling. That is one option but is not always the best option.

It is interesting to note everyone is made up of three parts. We all have a body *(soma)*, a soul *(psuche)* and a spirit *(pneuma)* (1 Thessalonians 5:23). The body *(soma)* relates to our environment, the spirit *(pneuma)* relates to God. The soul *(psuche)* relates to those around us. The word for soul, *psuche*, is also called our *psyche* from which we get the word *psychology*.

The person who should have the best training to deal with soul problems is someone trained in helping people finding the balance and completeness between the body, soul and spirit. That is what a Minister is supposed to be trained to do. That is a specific part of a Pastoral Ministry.

There is also a professional or non-professional counseling ministry every church should have called *healing* (1 Corinthians 12:28; Galatians 6:1; Romans 15:14). A healing ministry, in this context, addresses inward healing of the spirit and soul, which can have a positive effect physically.

- When people need counseling in your church where do they go?
- What is the role of your Pastor in counseling?
- Do other people in your church counsel, other than the Pastor?
  If so, who else counsels?
- Do you train other people to counsel?
  If so, how are they trained?

## 18.  Special Programs & Other Ministries.

There are other programs and ministries than those already addressed. This is the place to address those.

- What other programs or ministries does your church conduct?
- Are there particular ministries your church endorses or does not endorse, such as: *AWANA, Word of Life, Child Evangelism Fellowship, Gideons, Christian Businessmen's, Alcoholics Anonymous*, etc.
- Do you allow other ministries to meet in your church?
  If so who approves this?
  Under what conditions may they meet in your church?
- Who oversees other ministries in your church?

O     Who determines if other ministries are added?

## 19. Cooperative Evangelism, Fellowship & Ecumenical Services.

Some churches belong to a denomination, some to a fellowship or organization of churches. Some churches are independent but informally fellowship with other churches in their region, state or community. There are different levels of participation between churches.

### What is Your Position on the Following:

O     Is your church part of a denomination?

O     Is your church part of an association of churches such as the *Baptist Bible Fellowship? The General Association of Regular Baptist Churches? The Southern Baptist Convention? Independent Fundamental Churches of America?*

O     Do you believe in cooperating with other churches for evangelism, fellowship, outreach or in joint services?
If so, or not, what are your guidelines?
Some examples to address are:
- Pastor's Fellowships
- Men's, Women's or Youth conferences or activities
- Concerts
- Evangelistic Crusades, etc.

O     Do you participate in any way with coordinated ministries like: *National Day of Prayer, Samaritan's Purse, Operation Christmas Child,* etc.?

## 20. Missions.

Missions are a vital part of a church's responsibility to fulfill the Great Commission (Matthew 28:19-20; Mark 16:15).

O    Are there types of missions your church will support and ones you will not?

O    Are missionaries supported as a line item in the budget or through designated giving?

O    Do you use Faith Promise giving?
If so, what do you mean by this?

O    Do you participate in any kind of cooperative program?

O    Do you have an Annual Missions Conference?

O    How do you determine what missionaries can come speak in your church?

O    How do you determine whether or not your church will support a missionary?

O    How often do you review your missionary support and determine whether to continue, increase, or stop support for a missionary?

O    How do you determine how much you will support a missionary for?
Do you have a set minimum and/or maximum?

O    Do you start missionaries as prayer supported then later move them to financially supported?

O    How do you keep in touch with your missionaries?

O    How do you help your missionaries celebrate their birthdays, anniversaries, Christmas and other special days?

O    How do you keep your people informed about your missionaries?
Do you have a place where you post missionary updates?

O    Do you have an *adopt a missionary* type program where either individuals, small groups or Sunday School classes can take the responsibility to keep in touch with missionaries and keep your church informed?

❍ How do you keep people informed regarding the need for world missions?

❍ How do you encourage your people to become missionaries?

❍ Do you encourage your people to take missions exposure trips or to go on a short-term missions trip?
If so, how do you do this?
Where have they gone?

## 21. Baptism.

Every church has the responsibility to baptize people (Matthew 28:19-20). Who a church baptizes and how are they baptized differs between churches.

❍ By what mode do you baptize?
Immersion?

❍ What are the requirements for baptism?

❍ Do you accept baptisms from other churches?
If so, which ones do you accept and which do you not accept?

❍ Is there an age limit to get baptized?

❍ Do you baptize infants?

❍ What is your policy regarding baptizing minors.

❍ Where do you baptize?

❍ How often do you baptize?

## 22. Church Membership.

Besides being spiritual organizations, churches are legal entities with a membership structure.

❍ How does someone become a member of your church?

❍ Do the Pastor and his family automatically become members?

❍ Do you allow dual membership?

Can people be members of your church and another church at the same time? Some churches allow this for Pastors and Missionaries.

○ Is there an age limit to become a member?

○ Do you have a distinction between **Voting Members** and **Non-Voting Members**?

Many churches have a distinction between those members who may vote and those who may not. Some call those who can vote, **Voting Members**, others call them **Active Members**.

Some churches have a policy all members are able to vote unless they are officially informed they are an **Inactive Member**. If you church has this policy you are open to some dangers unless you carefully follow the notification procedure. Many churches have members who do not attend, and who have not been informed they are inactive, yet they come to important business meetings to cast a vote.

Some churches adopted the policy that when people become members it does not automatically mean they can vote. In some churches, voting is a privilege earned by faithful attendance and supporting the church financially. Hence, rather than having to inform members they are **Inactive Members**, which is a negative experience, **Voting Member** status is *earned* through faithful attendance and supporting the church. Rather than keeping a **Voting Member** role, voting is done on an, *on your honor* system, with the right of challenge. Under that model, all members can participate in the life of the church, but only **Voting Members**, those who attend the church and support it financially, are the ones who vote on the business of the church. That position eliminates many problems.

○ Do you maintain a list of the different types of members *(Active, Inactive, Voting, etc.)*?

O    Are people notified which type of membership they hold?
If so, how do you notify them?

O    Do you accept, or grant, transfers of membership?
If so, what are the conditions?

## 23.   Communion – The Lord's Supper.

Most churches celebrate communion, also referred to as the Lord's Supper. This is an area where there are various opinions and methods as to how it should be observed.

O    What is your position on Communion?

O    Who may take Communion?
-   Is it for all Believers?
-   Is it for just a Specific Group of Believers?
-   Is it only for people who attend your church?
-   Is it only for members?
-   Is there an age restriction?

O    How often do you observe Communion?

O    Who is involved in serving Communion?

O    Do you use unleavened bread *(matzo)*?

O    Do you use unfermented wine *(grape juice)*?

## 24.   Church Finances.

Church finances are a challenge because unlike a business, which charges for its services, a church depends on the willing donations of its members and attendees. Church offerings tend to fluctuate and can be easily impacted by many factors.

It takes a lot of wisdom to handle church finances properly. It is very important to carefully plan and have impeccable financial accountability. Many churches have ended up in serious legal problems because they do not have clearly defined financial policies.

O    What method do you believe God uses to support His Church?

❍ What is your position on fund raising, bake sales, etc.?

❍ Do you believe every believer should give God the minimum of the tithe (*firstfruits* Proverbs 3:9)?

❍ Do you believe the tithe should be given through the Local Church?

❍ How, and when, do you provide people the opportunity to worship the Lord with their tithes and offerings?

❍ Do you use offering envelopes?

❍ Do you have a method people can use for automatic giving through their bank?

❍ How do you handle designated giving?
Do you ever use designated funds for other purposes?
What do you do if you cannot, in good faith, allocate funds designated for a specific purpose?

❍ What accountability do you have for counting the offering?

❍ Who may know specifically what people are giving?

❍ Do you believe it is biblically acceptable for the church to borrow money?
If so, what do you believe it is acceptable to borrow for, and what Scripture do you base that on?

❍ Do you draft and approve an Annual Operating Budget which becomes a guide and authorization for spending?
How is this prepared and when is it approved?

❍ How do you update your church on offerings, in comparison to the budget?

O How do you authorize spending items which exceed, or are not specified, in the budget?

O How many signatures do you have on church accounts?
Who signs?

O Who determines if a Special Offering or Love Offering is to be received?

O Do you have a Benevolence Fund to help people with emergencies or pressing needs?
- How is this budgeted?
  How is this replenished?
- How do you determine who receives funds from this?
- What are the guidelines for distributing these funds?
- Who administers this?

O How do you teach your people the Biblical principles of finances?

## 25. Church Business.

Though the church is a spiritual organization and is accountable to God for how it conducts its business, it is also accountable to its people and in most places is subject to some government regulations.

It is important to clarify how you conduct the business of the Church.

O Are you incorporated by the state?

O Are you familiar with state laws regarding your church?

O How do you keep updated about changes in the laws, which effect you?

O What Church Officers do you have?

O What training is provided for Church Officers?

O What are the duties of each Church Officer?

○    Do you have insurance to protect those who serve as Church Officers?

○    How are your Church Officers chosen?

○    How long do they serve?

○    Are there term limits for Church Officers?

○    What officers make up the Church Board?

○    How often, and when, does the Church Board meet?
      How long do the meetings normally last?

○    Who moderates the Church Board meetings?

○    How often do you have church business meetings?
      When are they held and how long do they normally last?

○    How do you determine what is addressed at church business meetings?

○    Do you use a written agenda for your meetings?
      Who puts together the agenda?
      When is the agenda made available?

○    What voting percentage is needed for an item to pass in a business meeting?

○    Who moderates your church business meetings?

○    How do you call a special church business meeting?

○    What office equipment does your church have?

○    Do you have a church website?
      What Social Media do you use?
      Who sets it up, updates it and maintains it?
      Who determines what goes on it?

○    Do you have internet access?
      If, so, what kind?

## 26.    Church Staff (Paid & Volunteer).

Every church has people who carry out the work of the church. Some may be paid, but many are volunteers. You need clearly defined policies regarding church staff.

O    Do you have standard qualifications, polices, practices and personal standards for workers?
For example, are there any positions, paid or volunteer, a person does not have to be a member of your church to hold, such as janitor?
Are there certain practices workers must abstain from, such as the use of alcohol?

O    How often are policies, procedures and standards for staff reviewed, and by whom?

O    Who determines who fills a service position in your church?

O    Who determines the need for paid church staff?

O    Do you have an organizational flow chart?

O    If staff are needed, how are staff chosen and approved?

O    How are staff salaries and responsibilities determined?

O    Who oversees staff and who do staff answer to?

O    Do you have any secretarial staff?
What are their roles and duties?

## 27.   Marriage, Divorce & Remarriage.

Marriage, divorce and remarriage are very controversial issues. Be sure you know where you as a church, and where a Prospective Candidate, stand on these issues so you do not have a major conflict later.

O    Who may be married in your church building?

O    Do you allow your facilities to be used for weddings by people outside your church?

O    What are the requirements for someone to be married by your Pastor?

O    What is your position on same sex marriage or civil unions?

O    What is your position on cohabitation before marriage?

❍ May the Pastor conduct a wedding for a believer and an unbeliever?

❍ May the Pastor conduct a wedding for two non-believers?

❍ Are there people the Pastor may marry, but not in your church?

❍ Do you require pre-marital counseling before a couple is married?

❍ What is your position on divorce and remarriage?

❍ Are there biblical grounds for divorce?
What are they?

❍ Are there biblical grounds for re-marriage?
What are they?

❍ Are there positions in your church a divorced person may not hold?

## 28.  Schools.

A number of churches, even small ones, have Pre-School, Day Care or Parochial Schools. In some cases, those schools help significantly with church expenses and help underwrite the cost of church staff. Perhaps your church does not offer these services, but you should determine if that might be a possibility in the future.

❍ Do you have a Pre-School or Day Care Program?
If you do, what does it entail, who works in it and who may attend?

❍ Does your church have a Christian Day School?
If you do, what grades do you offer, who works in it, who may attend? How is it supported?

❍ What is your position on Christian Schools vs. Public Schools?

❍ How do you feel about Home Schooling?

❍ Are there particular colleges you endorse or encourage your students to attend or not to attend?

## 29.    Funerals & Cremation.

Everyone in your church is going to die, hopefully not at the same time. There is usually a funeral or memorial service for those who die.

Significant changes are taking place in this area. Years ago, almost everyone had their funeral at a church and was buried in a cemetery. Now many people are bypassing the church and having their funerals at a funeral home.

Just a few decades ago, hardly anyone was cremated. Many churches believed cremation was wrong. They followed the Jewish tradition of burying their dead. They also drew a parallel to Christ who was buried, and taught his followers should also be buried. Most however did not use borrowed tombs for their burials, and unlike Christ, they stayed in their graves for more than three days.

If you were cremated, years ago, many churches would not allow you to have a funeral or memorial service in their building. In 1983, the Catholic Church changed its position and began to allow cremation. That rapidly had an impact on attitudes and practices. Other churches also changed. Cremation is now the most common method.

Death is very emotional issue. What is your church's position on this?

O    Who may have a funeral or memorial service in your church?

O    Do you have a position on cremation?

O    Do you have a Church Cemetery?
     If so, who administers the Cemetery?
     Are their restrictions who may be buried there?
     How is it maintained?

## 30.    Politics.

Christianity played an important role in the founding of America. For the first 100 years, many elected officials were ministers or people trained in schools founded to train ministers. Christianity had a major positive influence in both government and school until the 1950's when the religion of *Secular Humanism* replaced Christianity.

Some churches today believe Christians should not be involved in politics. Others believe it is a spiritual and moral responsibility to be involved. What is your church's position?

O What is the role of the Church and Christians in politics?
Some churches, such as *Thomas Road Baptist Church* in Lynchburg, VA., and ministries, like *Wallbuilders* and *Focus on the Family* have been at the forefront of the political arena in moral areas. What is your church's position on that?

O What level of participation in the political process is acceptable, or not acceptable, for a Pastor, church or individual Christian?

O A church should not endorse a political Candidate but can staff publically support a particular Candidate as long as they do not promote them in church?

O Can a Pastor, or church staff member hold political office?

## 31. Community Involvement.

Many churches believe community involvement is part of its responsibility to fulfill the second part of the *Great Commandment* (Matthew 22:35-40). Christ said we are to love our neighbors as ourselves. He also said when we help those in need we are ministering to Him (Matthew 25:31-46).

Community involvement can take many shapes and forms. Many churches participate in town events, celebrations and parades.

Community involvement can also extend to being involved with more impending things such as helping others during times of disaster. When disaster strikes Mennonites, Baptists, Catholics, and even the Amish *(known for their separation from society)*, along with those from many other churches, are often there to help others. Most people are unaware, whenever there is a disaster, the *Southern Baptist Disaster Relief Ministry* is there to help as one of the three agencies working with the United States Department of Homeland Security.

- ○ How is your church involved in the life of your community?

- ○ Do you help your community by participating in community projects like Disaster Relief, *Red Cross, Habitat for Humanity*, etc.?

## 32. Moral & Social Issues.

Many churches have always been involved speaking out about various moral and social issues. Churches led the fight to end slavery and discrimination.

Where does your church stand on the following issues?

- ○ Abortion
- ○ Birth Control
- ○ Adoption
- ○ Pre-Marital Cohabitation
- ○ Same Sex Marriage
- ○ Polygamy
- ○ Stem Cell Research
- ○ Euthanasia

## 33. Pastoral Policies.

Each church is responsible to take care of its Pastor. The Bible says in 1 Timothy 5:17, a Pastor who serves well deserves a double salary. Some churches would like to provide more to their Pastor but are not able. Some do not provide enough.

Your church's policies about how you pay your Pastor and what benefits you provide are very important. Sometimes a Candidate would like to accept a call but is unable to accept the compensation a package a church offers because it does not meet his family's needs.

Make sure your church adequately addresses the following:

O How is the Pastor paid?

O Which of the following is provided for the Pastor and how?
- Salary
- Retirement
- Housing Allowance or Equity Position *(if you have a Parsonage)*
- Phone Allowance
- Ministry Car or Car Allowance
- Medical Insurance
- Day School Tuition *(if there are children)*
- Continuing Education Allowance & Policy
- Conference Expenses
- Book Allowance
- Missions Trips
- Vacations
- Sabbatical Policy
- Moving Expenses

O How are vacations determined?

O What type of schedule do you expect of your Pastor?

O How often will the salary and benefits be reviewed?

O What do you expect of the Pastor's wife?

O Do you provide compensation for the Pastor's wife?

# Determine the Qualifications for Your Pastor

## What is a Pastor?

Before a church can begin a search for a Pastor it must answer this question, *What is a Pastor?*

A good preliminary exercise is to have each person in your church *(both members and attendees, of all ages)* write out the answer to that question.

After they write out their answer, ask them to write a description of, *The Pastor We Would Like.* Those answers will give the Pastoral Search Committee a lot of insight into what the people are thinking. Those should be helpful in identifying perceived needs but should not be the final guidelines in seeking a Pastor.

First, you must review the Biblical Qualifications for a Pastor (1 Timothy 3:1-7 and Titus 1:5-9). These must be adhered to strictly with no exceptions, as they come directly from Scripture. When you are not sure about a qualification, take the more conservative position and you will be sure not to go wrong.

In addition to the Biblical qualifications, there are a number of other issues I strongly recommend you address.

## Some Important Distinctions.

You must understand two important distinctions before you can consider calling someone to serve as Pastor of your church:

1.    The difference between a **Pastoral Ministry** and **Being a Pastor**.

The Bible lists five categories of **Occupational Ministries** in Ephesians 4:11. One of those categories is **Pastoral Ministry**. You can have Pastoral Ministry yet not be the Pastor of a Church.

2.    The difference between a person's **Spiritual Gift** and **Ministry.**

## Spiritual Gifts & Selecting a Pastor

Understanding Spiritual Gifts plays a very important part in finding a Pastor. Being a Pastor is not a Spiritual Gift, it falls under one of the five categories of **Occupational Ministries**, God gives to the churches (Ephesians 4:11). A person with any one of the Spiritual Gifts may be used by God in a Pastoral Ministry. That is addressed later in this book.

A Pastor's Spiritual Gift will give them a unique *perspective* on how they fulfill their ministry. Depending on which gift they have, they will approach Pastoral ministry from that *perspective*. They will bring with them, their own strengths and weaknesses. Understanding the Biblical teaching on Spiritual Gifts will help you understand why Pastors can be so different. I recommend my books, *Unraveling the Holy Spirit Controversy,* and *Understanding People By Means of Their Spiritual Gift.*

The Bible says we must understand what God says about Spiritual Gifts (1 Corinthians 12:1). The following presents a brief summary of some important points to consider about Spiritual Gifts as you seek to find the Right Pastor. In the introductory passage on Spiritual Gifts, in 1 Corinthians 12:4-6, God gives us an important outline. He says there is a difference between:

○    Our **Gift** (v. 4).

○    Our **Ministry** (Administration) (v. 5).

○    And the **Results** (Operations) (v. 6).

Our Spiritual **Gift** is **who we are.** Our gift gives us a unique *perspective* and *potential* for service. The **Ministries** are **where we use our gift.** The **Results** are **sovereignly given by God.** Our Gift does not change, our Ministry may. We do not have to worry about the Results, God gives them as He see fit.

○ The **Gifts** are listed in one place
Romans 12:6-8

> Having then gifts differing according to the grace that is given us, whether **prophesy**, let us prophesy according to the proportion of faith; or **ministry**, let us wait on our ministering: or he that **teacheth**, on teaching; or he that **exhorteth**, on exhortation: he that **giveth**, let him do it with simplicity; he that **ruleth**, with diligence; he that **sheweth** mercy, with cheerfulness.
>
> Romans 12:6-8

**The Giver** – Their joy is coming up with ideas, and the resources to bring their ideas into reality.

**The Ruler** – Their joy is organizing something. They keep the overview and do not want to get bogged down with details.

**The Teacher** – Their joy is gathering information. They like details and can overwhelm you with those details.

**The Prophet** – Their joy is identifying right and wrong and convincing others.

**The Mercy Person** – Their joy is comforting people and seeing needs are met.

**The Ministry Person** – Their joy is doing a job. They need to know the details about what to do. They can get sidetracked doing something.

**The Exhorter** – Their joy is encouraging others so a job gets completed. They are very results oriented.

○    The **Ministries** are listed in two places because there are **Two Major Categories of Ministry**:

**The 8 (Eight) Ministries Every Church Should Have:**

And God hath set some in the church, first **apostles**, secondarily **prophets**, thirdly **teachers**, after that **miracles**, then **gifts of healings, helps, governments, diversities of tongues**.

1 Corinthians 12:28

**The 5 (Five) Ministries Given to Benefit More Than One Church:**

And He gave some **apostles**; and some, **prophets**; and some, **evangelists**; and some **Pastors** and **teachers**.    Ephesians 4:11

○    The **Results** are listed in one place.
1 Corinthians 12:6-10

God gives a variety of different results to different people, when people use their Gift in a Ministry.

And there are diversities of operations, but it is the same God which worketh all in all. But the manifestation of the Spirit is given to every man to profit withal. For to one is given by the Spirit the **word of wisdom**; to another the **word of knowledge** by the same Spirit; to another **faith** by the same Spirit; to another the **gifts of healing** by the same Spirit; to another the **working of miracles**; to another **prophesy**; to another **discerning of spirits**; to another **divers kinds of tongues**; to another **the interpretation of tongues**.

1 Corinthians 12:6-10

# Causes of Confusion in Relation To Spiritual Gifts.

### 1.     Confusion Occurs When We Do Not Clearly Make the Distinctions God Makes, Concerning the Gifts, Ministries and Results.

Too often people make the mistake of ignoring the outline God gave in 1 Corinthians 12:4-6 and refer to Ministries or Results as Gifts. God says we must not do that (1 Corinthians 12:1).

> Now concerning spiritual *gifts* [***pneumatikon***], brethren, I would not have you ignorant [***agnoein***].
> *1 Corinthians 12:1*

### 2.     Confusion Comes When We Fail to Make the Distinction Between the Gifts, Ministries and Results With the Same Name.

There is a *Gift of Teaching* (Romans 12:7) and a *Ministry of Teaching*. There is also a *Ministry of Teaching* **within** a church (1 Corinthians 12:28) and a professional *Ministry of Teaching* given to be used in **more than one church** (Ephesians 4:11). That causes confusion if people do not clearly identify the differences.

You do not need to have the *Gift of Teaching* to be a *Teacher*. When you do a study on the Gifts you will learn the person with the Gift of Teaching finds their greatest joy in the learning process, not necessarily in telling others what they learned.

The root of the Greek word for teacher (***didasko***) is ***dao***, which means **to learn**. A person with the Gift of Teaching is primarily *one whose greatest joy is learning.* They love to gather lots of facts and information. They are a very detailed person. They often have a hard time being concise because they see all truth as important. Romans 12:7, addresses the

Teacher's weakness and says the Teacher needs to teach others.

Have you ever heard people say, we need a Pastor with the Gift of Teaching? Do they really want a Pastor with the Gift of Teaching (Romans 12:7) or do you want one who can effectively fulfill the Ministry of Teaching (Ephesians 4:11)?

## 3.    Confusion Comes When People Make the Mistake of Speaking of a Person Having More Than One Gift.

The Bible warns against saying a person has more than one gift (1 Corinthians 12:3-5). Our Gift (*charismaton)* is part of what makes us *who* **we are**. Our Gift is *the thing which gives us our greatest joy* (*chara*). It gives us our **unique perspective** on life. Each of us have only one gift (1 Timothy 4:14; 1 Peter 4:10). God makes this clear by using the analogy of a physical body to parallel our Spiritual Gift (1 Corinthians 12; Romans 12). Each of us are one part of the body. You cannot be a foot and a mouth. Sometime you may be a foot in a mouth.

Our gift makes us a unique part of the local body of believers. Each part of the body does some things better than other parts. For example, hands are the best part of the body for writing, but if your hands do not work properly, you can write with your mouth or even your feet, though that is more difficult. Though the feet can do hand things, it does not make them hands. The same is true with Spiritual Gifts and Ministries. People with the gift of Ruling/Administration (Romans 12:8) can do the Ministry of Teaching, but that does not mean they have the Gift of Teaching (Romans 12:7). Their **Gift is who they are**, their joy, their motivation. Their **Ministry is what they do**.

## 4.    Confusion Comes From People in Ministry Who Mean Well.

Some Pastors, who have an effective Teaching Ministry, sometimes refer to themselves as a **Pastor-Teacher**. They put together the last two Occupational Ministries listed in

Ephesians 4:11. Some people think they are linked together, yet in Scripture they are two distinct ministries. All Pastors must teach, but not all Pastors have the Gift of Teaching, nor are they required to have that gift.

# Determine Personal Qualifications For a Pastor

In addition to the Biblical Qualifications for a Pastor, it is important to look at a Candidate's personal qualifications as reflected in the following areas. Many of these areas are very personal. Having a Candidate answer these questions will help you know more about the person who will be entrusted with the care of your souls. I recommend you ask the Prospective Candidate all these questions. It is best to include these on a questionnaire and then ask for clarification of any of them in person.

## 1. His Family Life.

O   What place does his family have in his life?

O   Does he have a good relationship with his wife?

O   Does he, or his wife, have a previous marriage?

O   How does he view the role of a Pastor's wife?

O   Does he rule his house well?

O   What type of relationship does he have with his children?

O   How does he feel about discipline and corporal punishment?

O   Are any of his children not following the Lord?

O   Does his family really like your area?

○ Does he feel his children must attend Christian School?

○ Does he have a tradition to go visit family, which are in a different geographic area from yours around holidays, such as Christmas or Thanksgiving or at other specific times of year?

## 2. His Personal Life.

Some of these questions may not seem important, but the answers to these questions will tell you a lot about a person.

○ What is his format for his own personal devotions?

○ What are his hobbies?

○ What type of weekly schedule does he have now?

○ What type of a weekly schedule would you expect him to keep?
How flexible is that?

○ Does he have a written personal budget?

○ Are his finances current?
Is he in debt?

○ Which books does he use most?

○ What are the three websites he visits most frequently?

○ What are three of his favorite television shows?

○ What are three of his favorite movies?

○ Who are three of his favorite musicians?

○ What are three of his all-time favorite books?

○ What are three magazines he reads?

○ What are three material things he would like to have?

○ Who are three people he respects most? Who in the ministry?

○ Where does he get his world and national news from?

❍   Who are his favorite sports teams?

❍   Where does he get his advice from?

❍   How often does he fast?

## 3.   His Educational & Professional Background.

❍   Where did he attend school?
When and for how long?
Ask for a copy of his transcripts.

❍   What courses did he take?

❍   What degrees or certificates does he hold?

❍   What background does he have in Biblical languages *(Hebrew & Greek)*?

❍   What Greek version does he think is most reliable?

❍   What Bible version(s) does he use for teaching and preaching?
For personal study?

❍   What is his attitude toward education?

❍   What course of self-improvement has he sought since graduation from Bible College or Seminary?

❍   What is his current plan for self-improvement? Does this include any formal continuing education?

❍   What is his Christian Service record: before entering the ministry; while in college and seminary, and between positions?

❍   What Christian employment has he held?
Ask for a complete employment record, leaving no gaps from college graduation to present.
Who did he answer to on each job?
What is his record of accomplishments on each job *(Does he stress people or programs)?*

❍   What are his long-term personal goals?
Watch out for vague statements such as, *to do the will of God.*

○ What is his preaching style?

○ What training and experience does he have in the area of Pastoral Counseling?

○ What training and experience does he have in Church Administration?

○ What training and experience does he have in Christian Education?

○ What specific classes and ages has he taught? What specific classes and ages does he prefer to teach?

○ What is his teaching style?

○ What training does he have in Evangelism and Soul-Winning?

○ Ask him to share three of his more recent soul-winning experiences.

○ Does he use a basic soul-winning plan? What is it?

○ Does he have a Personal Statement of Faith and Standard of Conduct?

○ Has he written or published any articles, books or other items?

○ Was he ordained? Is so, when, where and by whom?

○ What does he see as the purpose and format for each of the following:
- Sunday School
- Morning Service
- Evening Service
- Mid Week Service

○ What discipleship training does he have?

○ What method(s) does he use to disciple a New Believer?

○ What training and experience does he have in the area of Youth Work?

○ What training and experience does he have in the area of music?

# Determine the Procedure for Considering & Calling a Candidate

Each church must determine an official procedure for considering a Candidate. The procedure you propose must be officially approved by your church.

## Suggested Candidating Procedure.

The Pastoral Selection Procedure has some similarities to the procedure a company uses to find and hire a new employee but there are significant differences. It is more like the procedure a company uses to hire a new Chief Executive Officer, but still has some significant differences.

Much of the material in this book was written years ago in a manual format as a practical tool for Pastoral Search Committees. Though most Pastoral Search Committees mean well, most are unfamiliar with Pastoral Etiquette. It is an area where most people never receive training. There is a proper and ethical way to conduct the candidating procedure.

The following is a recommended procedure, based on both professional and Pastoral Etiquette and many years of assisting churches. Each church must decide its own procedure.

### 1. A Recommendation Form is Required.

No Candidate shall be considered until someone submits a Recommendation Form to consider them as a Candidate.

### 2. Only One Candidate Shall Be Considered at a Time.

Unlike a company, which looks for numerous job applicants, conducts interviews and then makes a choice, the search for a Pastor is different. Although the church does conduct business, it is not a business, it is a church. The search for a Pastor is more like an individual seeking a spouse than a company seeking an employee. See the section, **The Romantic Parallel**, at the beginning of this book.

The church is a supernatural organism of which Christ is the head. If you believe in a sovereign God, then you realize God has one specific man whom He would have for the position of Pastor in your church. Nowhere in Scripture does God send out numerous applications, set up interviews and then pick the man for the job. In that way, God's wisdom is different from the world's wisdom.

If you are convinced there is one right man for your church, then pray God will show you that man. When a name is put forward to consider, make it a matter of prayer and determine yes or no, before going on to another name. If numerous names are all presented at once, pray over them, without going through all their details and determine one man to consider. Do not accept applications or make phone calls regarding more than one man at a time. That is unethical.

### 3.     Inform Any Person Filling the Pulpit if They Are Candidate.

The Pastoral Search Committee shall not speak with, nor invite anyone to speak in the church, whom they are possibly considering as a Potential Candidate, unless they have clearly informed the person they are a Candidate.

### 4.     When a Prospective Candidate is Identified.

**O     If He is Currently Pastoring a Church.**

One or two members of the Pastoral Search Committee shall go hear a Prospective Candidate speak. They shall not, at that time, tell anyone in that other church they are there seeking a Pastor.

After they hear the Prospective Candidate speak, they shall report to the Pastoral Search Committee with a recommendation to proceed to consider them, or to look at someone else. If the committee decides to proceed, then complete this step, sending them the packet, as you would for **Someone Not Currently Pastoring a Church.**

Inform the Candidate, if they are interested in being considered as a Candidate, they do not have to inform their current church, nor should they submit reference forms to leaders in their church, until after the first pulpit visit to your church. If, after that first visit to your church, you both decide to proceed, then they shall inform their church and submit reference forms to leaders in their church. Remember this is a first step and it is possible it will not proceed any further. They should not inform their church unless it proceeds.

O **If They Are Not Currently Pastoring a Church**

Send them a Candidate Package to help them determine if they would like to be considered as a Candidate.

# The Candidate Package

## Include the following in the Candidate Package:

- Questionnaire.
- Reference Request Forms.
- A Brief History and Profile of Your Church.
- The Church Constitution & By-Laws.
- A Profile of the Community with relevant demographics.
- A Tentative Job Description, with an explanation it will be customized with the Pastor you call.
- The Church's Candidating Procedure.

- Basic Information regarding the proposed Compensation plan, which is subject to negotiation.

This package should **NOT** include the Church's Positions and Practices, which the Pastoral Search Committee identified. If you provide the positions first, it will bias their answers. The **Questionnaire** will help you see where they stand on all those issues and help you see if they are compatible with where you stand. It is unlikely anyone will match yours 100%.

I think it is advisable to tell Prospective Candidates *our church does not have a position on some of the issues addressed in the Questionnaire, but we know some of the issues are important to some people and we want to know what your position is, or if you do not have a position, on any of the issues.* Do not give them any indication which issues are important to you and which are not, at this time. You need to know where they stand. They may have some strong positions, which are not compatible with yours.

Ask the Prospective Candidate to respond with a written reply, either turning down the offer, or completing the Questionnaire within two weeks of receiving the letter. In *addition* to the letter, he may also respond by phone.

If you do not receive a response in two weeks, a member of the Committee shall call him to see the status. Unless there is some compelling reason, it is not a good sign if a Prospective Candidate takes too long to fill out requested information.

## 5.    Prayerfully Review the Questionnaire & References.

The Pastoral Search Committee shall not submit any name to the Church to approve as a Candidate, nor shall they invite a Potential Candidate to speak, until they conduct a *prayerful* and *careful* review of the completed questionnaire from the Candidate, as well as review and contact all his references.

Each person on the Committee should carefully read the questionnaire and make note of any questions, concerns, or positive things they observed.

After that review, the Pastoral Search Committee should discuss the results of everyone's evaluation as a group. If there are questions or concerns, which the Committee feels they need answered; assign two people the responsibility to place a conference call to the Potential Candidate to discuss the matter.

Once you have all questions or concerns answered, if the Committee is not interested in pursuing the Prospective Candidate, inform them in writing of your decision not to consider them as a Candidate.

If you do have the interest to proceed, this next step is very important. The Bible warns there is a spiritual battle and followers of the evil one will seek to become Pastors. They are like wolves who disguise themselves as sheep (Matthew 7:15). They will appear to be very good people, perhaps they may seem like a refreshing *Angel of Light* ( 2 Corinthians 11:14). I must sadly report I know of too many instances of deception by Prospective Candidates. You must do a thorough background check on any Potential Candidate you consider.

**Assign People on the Committee to *Contact* and *Confirm* the following:**

O　　**Educational Institutions Listed** – To confirm degrees or attendance.

O　　**Ordaining Church or Body** - To confirm ordination.

O　　**Most Recent Employer** – To discuss recent employment.

O　　**Previous Relevant Employers** – To discuss previous employment.

O　　**References Provided** – To speak with each one personally.

O　　**Criminal Background Check** – Your church insurance company will usually have a recommended provider for this service at a discounted price.

O     **Online Search** –To do an online search for anything related to the person.

The person, or people assigned to review the references, should personally call each of the references. Remember people usually provide only the names of people who will give them a good recommendation. Feel free to ask those references any additional questions.

Take good notes of any comments. It is usually a good idea to ask this question, *Is there anything you think we should know about this Candidate?*

Ask each person, given as a reference, to please provide the names and contact information of three other people who know the Prospective Candidate. Then send a **Confidential Reference Form** to each of those additional references. Ask them to return it to the Committee, either physically or electronically. The people who followed through on making the relevant contacts should report to the Committee.

I am sorry to say I know people who provided educational references from institutions they never attended as well as other information, which when investigated, proved to be untrue.

One church called me very excited about the fact they called a Pastor who went to the same school I attended. I did not remember that person so I checked my yearbook and they were not there. I called the school. They told me that person applied for the Pastoral Studies program but they rejected him for that program because he was divorced. He had not let the church know he was divorced.

I called him instead of the person from the church who contacted me. After exchanging some pleasantries, I asked him what school he attended. He told me the name of my school. I asked what year he graduated. When he told me the year he graduated, I told him I attended that school and graduated in that class. He hung up the phone. Two days later, the man from the church, who originally called me, called again. He said the strangest thing happened. Their new Pastor did not turn up for a meeting he was supposed to attend, nor return any calls. They went to his house and found he moved out. Learn from this and verify information on applications.

The person who does the **Online Search** should do a basic and advanced search a using a search engine, such as **Google, Bing** or **WebCrawler** using the Prospective Candidate's name. This may reveal new stories, personal posts and former addresses (including who lived with him).

Do a *Google Image Search* for the Prospective Candidate. Just type their name in the *Google Search Bar*, plus the word *image*. Most likely the search will return many images. Most of the images will not be the person you are searching for, yet some may. Click on any image, which appears to be the person you are looking for. That will open a large image and provide a choice to *Visit Page*, where that image is displayed. Always visit those pages.

One such search revealed a Potential Candidate listed himself on a Dating Website, complete with his photograph, even though he was married.

Also, search on all Social Media, such as *Facebook* and *Twitter*. Look at their Posts, their Likes and their Friends lists. That may reveal a lot of information.

## 6.    Two Committee Members Shall Contact the Prospective Candidate.

After review of the completed questionnaire and references, assign two members of the Pastoral Search Committee to contact the prospect via conference call or personal visit or electronic messaging. Ask additional questions the Committee wants answered and request any other information they feel is necessary to make a proper decision.

After discussing any questions, and upon satisfactory answers, this may be a good time to discuss general details about the Job Description and general, but not specific details of the Basic Compensation Package. This will help determine if there is compatibility or significant differences between how he views the job of being a Pastor and what your church is looking for. That is also a good time for the Prospective Candidate to ask questions he feels he would like answered.

The Pastoral Search Committee should then meet after this interview to discuss the results. You may wish to schedule a conference call in advance, with the Prospective Candidate, and the Committee, to answer any additional questions.

## 7.    If the Prospective Candidate Does Not Pass the Review.

If the Prospective Candidate does not pass the review, you must drop him. Inform him by a letter stating the reason why you choose not to progress with him.

If someone in the church recommended the Candidate, it is a good idea to inform that person who made the recommendation of your decision, after the initial review. Inform them, that after you contacted the Prospective Candidate, a decision was made not to proceed any further. Specific reasons as to why someone did not pass the review shall remain confidential.

## 8.    If the Prospective Candidate Passes the Review.

If the Prospective Candidate passes the review, inform him by letter, and by phone, that he is officially a Candidate and the process will proceed.

This is a good time to remind him to review the Candidating Procedure, which you provided in the Candidate Package. That will help him see the next steps to come. It should help him understand, he is a Candidate but must pass a number of other steps before he can be approved to be the Pastor.

Make it clear to the Candidate you only consider one Candidate at a time. Let him know you are prayerfully and carefully seeking the *Right Pastor* God wants for your church. Let him know everything you are doing now is to determine whether or not he is that man.

Once someone becomes a Candidate, the Pastoral Search Committee must understand it may make recommendations to the church but the decision is then up to the Voting Members if the Candidate is to become their Pastor.

## 9.    Present the Candidate's Name and Profile to the Church.

Now it is time to officially, present the name of the Candidate, along with a brief profile, to the Church.

Members may submit any questions they have, regarding the Candidate, to the Pastoral Search Committee in writing.

Make it clear this is the beginning of the candidating process. Remind people, this is not a call for someone to become the Pastor, but to do a review to see if both the Candidate and the Church believe God wants them to be their Pastor. Let them know there will be some important meetings for them to attend, and that their input and vote is important.

## 10.    The Candidate Shall Come Speak in the Church.

Invite the Candidate to come speak at your church. It is advisable to have the Candidate speak at all services normally covered by the Pastor. If the Pastor of your church would normally teach Sunday School and preach in a Morning Service or any other service, have him speak at each of those.

He should be available after the service to stand around for a *meet and greet* with people, as a Pastor would normally do. This will help him and your people get acquainted. It is a good idea for the Pastoral Search Committee to observe how he interacts will the people.

## 11.    The Committee Meets Privately with the Candidate.

On the day the Candidate comes to speak, the Pastoral Search Committee should meet privately with the Candidate after he speaks. They should ask any additional questions. It might be nice to do this over dinner.

## 12. The Committee Meets After the Interview.

The Pastoral Search Committee should meet after the interview to discuss relevant items related to the interview.

The Committee may recommend further examination, or recommend not to pursue the Candidate any further or it may recommend the Church have the Candidate fill the pulpit again.

At this point, it is important the Committee remember it may not act without approval from the Church. The Committee should make its recommendations as a motion to the Church at a Special Business Meeting held for that purpose.

## 13. Hold a Special Business Meeting.

Schedule a Special Business Meeting, in advance, to take place no later than one week after the Candidate filled the pulpit. The Pastoral Search Committee shall present its recommendation whether the Church should continue to pursue the Candidate or not. People may ask questions.

## 14. The Church Shall Vote to Proceed or Not.

The Church shall vote at that meeting whether to proceed to pursue the Candidate or not. It is important everyone understands they are not voting to call the Candidate at that time, but on whether to proceed to the next step or not.

If the Congregation raises questions or concerns, the Committee needs to do follow-up work on before they vote to continue with the candidating process.

○ **If Additional Information is Requested.**

Schedule another business meeting. Inform the Candidate of that decision by a letter, and with a phone call. Request the additional information.

The Committee shall examine the response and present it to the Church at the next meeting. Then the Church will vote to proceed, or not, with the candidating procedure.

O    **If You Vote Not to Proceed with the Candidate.**
Inform the Candidate of the decision by a letter, and with a phone call, stating the reason.

O    **If You Vote to Proceed with the Candidate.**
The Pastoral Search Committee shall contact him by letter, and with a phone call, to inform him of the Church's continued interest and to schedule a follow-up date for the Candidate to return to speak.

## 15.    The Candidate Shall Customize the Job Description.

Ask the Candidate to customize the Preliminary Job Description, applying their gift and abilities within the context of your church. Ask them to also prepare their Philosophy of Ministry and explain how that is compatible with your church.

## 16.    The Candidate Shall Present His Philosophy of Ministry.

When the Candidate returns for the follow-up visit, provide him the opportunity to present his Philosophy of Ministry to your church, whether in Sunday School or in a regular church service, or in a special meeting all are invited to attend. This will give your church a better understanding of the Candidate.

## 17.    Hold a Question & Answer Session with the Church.

Schedule a Question and Answer Session for the day the Candidate returns to speak. Members may ask the Candidate questions. The Chairman of the Pastoral Search Committee shall moderate the meeting.

## 18.  Schedule a Special Business Meeting.

Schedule a Special Business Meeting, in advance, for no later than two weeks, after the Candidate's return visit, or whatever time frame is required in your **Church Constitution and By-Laws**.

## 19.  If the Church Votes Not to Call the Candidate.

If the Church votes not to call the Candidate, inform him by letter, and by phone, stating the reason. If the Church votes not to call him, you may not reconsider him as a Candidate.

## 20.  If the Church Votes to Extend a Call to the Candidate.

If the Church votes to extend the call to the Candidate, the Church shall authorize the Pastoral Search Committee to finalize the Job Description and begin negotiations for a Compensation Package.

They shall contact the Candidate by letter and by phone and notify him of the decision. It is important for everyone to understand, though you extended the call, the Candidate is not the Pastor yet.

## 21.  The Committee Negotiates the Details with the Candidate.

The next step is for the Pastoral Search Committee to negotiate the Final Job Description and details of the Compensation Package. Depending on your current financial situation, you may need to consider a Graduated Compensation Plan, in which salary and benefits increase in stages.

There will be some cases, where you cannot work out the details and the Candidate cannot accept the call. This negotiation process may require a few special business meetings. The Church must approve a Compensation Package but it may provide the Committee broad parameters.

## 22. The Committee Presents the Results to the Church for Approval.

The Pastoral Search Committee must present the results of the negotiations to the church for final approval.

○ **If the Church Wants Changes to the Package.**

The Candidate shall be informed by letter, and by phone, stating changes the Church wants to the package.

Additional negotiations shall be conducted, until a final package is completed. That shall then be re-submitted to the Church for approval.

○ **If the Church Does Not Approve the Package.**

Inform the Candidate by letter, and phone, stating the reason the church did not accept the package. If the Church cannot approve a package, the Candidate does not become Pastor.

○ **If the Church Approves the Package.**

If the Church approves the package, the Church should authorize the Pastoral Search Committee to set the date for the **Installation** Service, where the Candidate officially becomes the Pastor.

## 23. Schedule the Installation Service.

The Pastoral Search Committee's last duty is to schedule an Installation Service for the new Pastor. This is addressed in detail in this book in the section called, ***The Installation Service.***

# Financial Considerations
## *Including Housing, Feeding & Hosting Candidates*

### 1. Expenses of the Pastoral Search Committee.

Expenses for operating a Pastoral Search Committee usually are not included in the normal church budget. The Pastoral Search Committee should propose an appropriation or reimbursement policy, to the Church, which the Church should vote on before the Committee incurs any expenditures.

### Some Expenses to Consider Include:

The following are expenses items the Pastoral Search Committee must consider, and estimate costs for, when submitting authorization to spend funds.

#### 1.1. Phone Calls.

There will be many long distance phone calls to Prospective Candidates and references.

#### 1.2. Correspondence.

There will be the need for stationary and postage.

#### 1.3. Trips to Hear Prospective Candidates.

If possible, reimburse the people on the Pastoral Search Committee for travel expenses associated with going to hear a Prospective Candidate.

Do not limit yourself to consider only Candidates who are nearby. I know of searches, which required Pastoral Search Committee members to drive or fly a long distance to hear a Prospective Candidate. The expense of going the distance paid off in finding the right Pastor.

#### 1.4. Housing and Compensating Candidates.

Housing and compensation for Candidates is addressed in more detail in this chapter. The expenses for Guest

Speakers or for an Interim Pastor are handled
differently than for a Pastoral Candidate.

## 2. Housing & Compensating Those Who Fill the Pulpit.

The following are proper, recommended remuneration
guidelines for guest speakers, musicians and others who come
to fill the pulpit or who conduct or participate significantly in
special meetings held in a church. The Church should elect to
determine specific remuneration figures and review such
figures annually.

Guest speakers and Candidates should be paid the same but
the way they are housed and fed differs significantly because
they are there for a different purpose. It is important to do what
is best, and proper, not just what is convenient.

### 2.1. Housing.

The purpose for having a guest speaker come, when
you are seeking a Pastor, is not the same purpose as
having a Candidate speak. The primary purpose of the
guest speaker, when you are seeking a Pastor, is to fill
the pulpit.

It is very likely you will have a number of guest
speakers during the time you are looking for a Pastor.
Though you may have your people house and feed
guest speakers at other times, to do that at this time puts
a strain on the pool of people you will need to host
Candidates.

Provide private housing *(not in homes)* for all guest
speakers, except Candidates. You may house guest
speakers in a nice self-contained Prophet's Chamber,
nice motel, or in a private guest room in the parsonage.
A room with a folding bed is unacceptable.

If you do not have any other options and must house a
guest speaker in a home, it is appropriate to consider
some compensation for the person housing them, for
saving your church the cost of a motel room.

## 2.2.   Meals.

Feeding guest speakers in homes is appropriate at other times, but while you are seeking a Pastor this can place a strain on people you will need to feed a Pastoral Candidate. Guest speakers (not Candidates), during the Pastoral Search, should have their meals at a restaurant. It is acceptable, but not required, for one or two members of the Pastoral Search Committee to eat with them to seek advice.

An amount should be budgeted and presented to guest speakers for having meals on their own. If you expect church staff, or others, to feed the guest speaker, provide them with a food allowance for this expense.

## 2.3.   Travel Expenses.

If possible, provide travel expenses for all speakers. This includes gas, tolls, meals and lodging, on the way to your church and back to their point of origin. Provide an appropriate amount designated for this purpose, separate from any honorarium.

If another church is included in the guest speakers circuit, the travel expenses should be pro-rated. You can provide, or negotiate, a mileage allowance and per diem allowance for meals, in lieu of actual expenses.

## 2.4.   Evangelists, Special Singers & Missionaries on Deputation.

These traveling ministries depend on the money they receive from ministering on a Sunday Morning for the bulk of their income.

For those in full-time professional Christian Service, the honorarium for ministering on a Sunday, should be the equivalent of the Pastor's weekly salary.

For services, they minister in, besides or in addition to Sunday, the honorarium should be about one-fourth (1/4) of the Pastor's weekly salary, for each additional day of service.

**2.5. Pastors, Missionaries on Furlough, Teachers, Lay Singing Groups, Those Who Travel Periodically and Staff from Other Ministries.**

People in those ministries have salaries or support and do not depend on the offerings for the bulk of their support. A respectable remuneration figure is one-fifth (1/5) of the Pastor's weekly service for each service they take part in. Sunday Morning's honorarium should be about two-fifths (2/5) of the Pastor's weekly salary.

**2.6. Love Offerings.**

It is best to budget remuneration for special speakers, not to take love offerings. Love offerings place an extra burden on your people.

You should only receive a Love Offering if there is a known genuine need, or if the Deacons or Trustees feel there is a need to provide additional remuneration above the amount budgeted for.

If you take a Love Offering, do it during the service, sometime after, never before, the person ministers.

# 3. Compensating Candidates.

You should pay a Candidate, following the same guidelines you use to pay a guest speaker,. Base the honorarium on the category of ministry they fall under *(see above)*. However, you should house and feed them differently.

The reason you are having a Candidate come is to get to know them and for them to get to know you. The best way for that to happen is to have them stay and eat in the homes of your people. That will necessitate your people being involved and willing to open their homes. It will also mean the Candidate will be more tired when they minister in the pulpit, but you and they will learn a lot more about each other if you do this.

**3.1. Housing.**

Even if you have a furnished parsonage, or prophet's chamber in your church, or reasonable accommodations nearby, in most cases it is best to house Candidates in the homes of church people. Though this is not recommended for other guest speakers, this is the best way to get to know a Candidate and for a Candidate to get to know your people.

Make sure you house them in a large enough home with a nice guest room or extra bedroom. A room with a folding bed is unacceptable.

Make sure you do not create any situations, which do not look appropriate. A male speaker should NEVER be in a home where another adult male is not present.

When a Candidate returns to speak, after their initial contact, they should bring their family with them. No matter how large their family is, in most cases it is still best to house them in the homes of your church people.

In some places, though housing and feeding Candidates in homes is best, culture has changed and in some areas it may be best to only feed them in member's homes.

## 3.2.    Meals.

If possible, the Candidate, and his family, should have all meals with church people. It is okay to have some meals at the church, with a larger group, and some with staff, or the Pastoral Search Committee but it is best for the Candidate to eat in people's homes or to go out for a meal with one or two families.

Many people who cannot house a Candidate can host them for a meal.

It is very important to ask a Candidate in advance about any food allergies, dietary requirements, as well as likes and dislikes. It may be inconvenient, but the effort will be well worthwhile.

## 3.3.    Travel Expenses.

If possible, provide travel expenses for all Candidates. Travel expenses should include gas, tolls, meals and lodging, on the way to your church and back to their point of origin. You could provide or negotiate a mileage allowance and a per diem allowance for meals in lieu of actual expenses.

### 3.4. Financial Compensation If the Candidate Has a Traveling Ministry.

Candidates who have a traveling ministry depend on the Sunday Morning offering for most of their income.

For those in full-time Christian Service, the honorarium for a Sunday, should be the equivalent of the Pastor's weekly salary. For services besides, or in addition, to Sunday, the honorarium should be about one-fourth (1/4) of the Pastor's weekly salary, for each additional day of service.

### 3.5. Financial Compensation for Candidates who are Presently Pastors, Missionaries on Furlough, Teachers, or Employed Some Other Way.

These ministries have salaries or support and do not depend on the offerings for the bulk of their support. A respectable remuneration figure is one-fifth (1/5) of the Pastor's weekly salary for each service in which they take part. Sunday Morning's honorarium should be about two-fifths (2/5) of the Pastor's weekly salary.

### 3.6. Love Offerings.

It is best to budget remuneration for special speakers. Only take a Love Offering if there is a genuine need, or if the Deacons or Trustees believe your church should provide additional remuneration above the amount budgeted. Receive this Love Offering during the service, sometime *after* the person ministers.

## 4. Determining a Pastor's Compensation Package.

Remember a Pastor's job has greater demands than a normal job. It is like a teacher, psychologist, coach, researcher, motivational speaker and president of a corporation, all rolled into one job.

The Bible says the ones which do a good job as Pastor deserve a double salary (1 Timothy 5:17). Too many churches do not properly address this. It is better to pay a Pastor more than less.

The financial needs of a Pastor vary greatly depending on their age, education, family and experience. The Church must be willing to negotiate the details of a Compensation Package depending on the individual and their circumstances.

God expects a man to provide for his family and to count the cost, before making major decisions (1 Timothy 5:8; Luke 14:28-30). Some Candidates may like to serve as your Pastor, but based on what you offer, they could not be your Pastor and meet the other obligations God has given them.

One method some churches use is to determine a compensation package is to offer the equivalent to a senior executive serving in your area, adjusted for varying levels of experience. If you are not presently able to offer that, you could present that type of package to a Candidate as your *goal*, but offer something less *immediately*, with plans for review and change as certain goals are met. The steps, to reach that package, will not be looked upon as raises. I know churches who did that. It can provide a good motivation for a Pastor who has faith in you to accept the call.

The following items should all be addressed in a compensation package. You may change any of these as you see fit. All items must be negotiated and then presented to your church for approval.

### 4.1. Salary.

Determine a yearly salary. You must determine if you pay this weekly, bi-weekly or monthly. Many churches pay staff on a weekly or bi-weekly basis.

## 4.2.  Retirement.

Is the Pastor part of the Social Security System? If he is, make sure you budget in those payments. If he is not, it is extra important to address his retirement, as he will not receive anything from the government for retirement based on his ministry.

## 4.3.  Housing Allowance or Equity Agreement.

The Church should provide either a parsonage and utilities, or if there is not a parsonage, a specific housing allowance

If the Pastor helps your church by staying in a parsonage, your church should consider drafting an *equity agreement* with the Pastor. That allows him to share in some of the equity he helps your church earn while he lives there.

## 4.4.  Phone Allowance.

If the Pastor and the Church share the same phone number, the Church should pay for the service. If the Pastor's home has a different line, which he will use for ministry, the Church should either pay for the Pastor's phone, or provide a phone allowance for the basic service and for ministry calls.

If your church wants the Pastor to have a cellular phone, it should provide one, which is to be used by the Pastor for ministry and have that billed to the Church.

## 4.5.  Ministry Car or Car Allowance.

Some churches provide their Pastor with a ministry car. The car either remains the property of the Church, or in some cases, may become the Pastor's property after a specified period.

If a ministry vehicle is not provided, a specified car allowance should be designated. That allowance is not considered income if it is carefully documented and used for gas, repairs and replacement due to ministry wear and tear on the car.

If your church is not able to provide a sufficient car allowance including anticipated replacement of the Pastor's vehicle, it should be willing to help financially when his vehicle wears out and needs to be replaced.

## 4.6.    Medical Insurance.

It is important to provide either medical insurance or a medical savings plan for the Pastor and his family. In America, the law requires this. You may find lower rates if you get coverage through Pastoral fellowships, associations or even the local Chamber of Commerce.

## 4.7.    Day School Tuition *(if there are children).*

If the Pastor believes his children should attend Christian School, or be Home Schooled, it is important to address that issue. Some churches provide a Day School Tuition allowance, other churches make an adjustment to the salary for this.

## 4.8.    Continuing Education Allowance & Policy.

Continuing education enhances a Pastor's ministry. Your church should adopt a continuing education policy to encourage the Pastor to continue his formal education. Studies should relate to his ministry in your church.

It is probably best to take one class at a time, as not to interfere with other duties. There are exceptions to that, such as some Doctor of Ministry or Ph.D. programs where the entire educational program revolves around the Pastor's ministry in your church.

The Church may elect to pay all, or part of the educational expenses. It is common to require a grade of B (3.0) or above for reimbursement.

## 4.9.    Conference Expenses.

The Church should encourage and try to help send the Pastor to conferences, which help improve his ministry skills.

It is recommended a Pastor attend one or two such conferences a year, at the church's expense. Attendance at such conferences is not considered vacation time.

### 4.10. Book Allowance.

The church may consider an annual book allowance for the Pastor to use toward acquiring ministry books.

### 4.11. Missions Trips.

The Church should encourage the Pastor to take periodic missions exposure trips, preferably to visit missionaries supported by your church. Your church should pay the expenses of said trips.

### 4.12. Vacations.

The Church should consider providing the Pastor with at least two weeks of paid vacation during each of the first two years he is with your church. Then, three weeks should be provided during each of the third through fifth years. After the fifth year, four weeks of paid vacation should be provided each year.

Pastors with previous Pastoral experience should be granted credit for time served in another Pastorate and may be allowed vacation time, consummate with experience, if approved by the Church.

Conferences, seminars and continuing education, are not vacation time.

It is important for the Pastor to take a vacation away from your church, therefore pay should not be taken in lieu of vacation, nor may vacation time accrue.

### 4.13. Sabbatical Policy.

It is customary, as well as a good idea, to offer your Pastor a professional Sabbatical.

After every ten years of ministry with your church, the Pastor should be allowed to apply to take a sabbatical of six months, with pay, in lieu of a vacation. Such sabbatical must have some type of ministry related, personal improvement or personal refreshment purpose.

### 4.14. Moving Expenses.

The Church should pay the expenses to move any Pastor they call, to your church.

### 4.15. Compensation for the Pastor's Wife.

If your church has duties it expects the Pastor's wife to perform it should consider compensation for her, or it should look at the Pastor's salary, as a family salary and increase it proportionately.

# 5. Severance Policy

Every church should have a Severance Policy. This provides specific policies for when a Pastor resigns or when a church asks a Pastor to leave. It is best to have this policy in place before calling a Pastor.

The following is a Recommended Severance Policy. Make sure a Prospective Pastor understands your policy.

O **Voluntary Resignation by the Pastor.**

The Pastor shall give sixty (60) days' notice if he plans to resign. After the date he completes his last sixty (60) days with full pay and benefits, the Pastor shall cease his duties. All benefits, during the notification period, will be pro-rated. A Pastor who chooses to leave prior to the 60-day termination notice shall forfeit any pay and benefits for that period.

Under this situation, the Pastor should be entitled to his pay for any unused vacation time from that year.

If a Pastor resigns, he should be responsible for all moving expenses. If there is a parsonage, and/or an office, the Pastor should be responsible for cleaning them before leaving.

○ **Involuntary Termination of the Pastor.**

After six months of continuous service with the church, if the church chooses to terminate the Pastor *(for reasons other than immorality, gross misconduct or severe dereliction of duties) (in accordance with such provisions in the Church Constitution and By-Laws regarding the necessary voting percentage required),* your church shall have obligations it must fulfill. After receiving notice, the Pastor shall continue to serve thirty days with full pay and benefits. He shall also receive two additional months of pay and benefits. In addition, it may be negotiated, in advance, to give him an additional one week of salary and benefits for each complete year served, up to a total of 20 additional weeks, as severance pay.

If he lives in a parsonage, he shall be given an additional 30 days, after his duties cease, to vacate the parsonage, for a total of 60 days from the date of the notice of termination. The board may elect to make the termination of duties effective immediately, but must pay the 30 day salary and benefits *(the period of the notice),* plus the two month's pay and benefits, plus any agreed upon severance pay or benefits. Under this situation, the Pastor is entitled to collect pay for any unused Vacation Time.

The Pastor will be allowed sixty (60) days from the date of the notice, to vacate the parsonage, or the Church may offer financial remuneration for early vacancy. Any occupancy of the parsonage, or storage of personal property, beyond the sixty (60) days, shall be subject to market rate rental.

Under this termination, the Church shall pay moving expenses and cleaning of the parsonage.

O   **Severe Termination of the Pastor.**

In the case of voluntary or involuntary termination for immorality, blatant impropriety, disgracing the cause of Christ, or reprobation, the Church shall act to make termination effective immediately. His duties shall cease immediately. He shall only receive thirty (30) days salary and benefits for the date of dismissal, plus any severance pay he earned, prior to any activity which warranted severe termination.

The Pastor will be allowed thirty (30) days to vacate the parsonage, from the date of the notice of dismissal, under the same conditions for Involuntary Termination.

The Pastor is entitled to pay for any unused Vacation Time from that year.

Under this situation, the Pastor is responsible for all moving expenses. If there is a parsonage, and/or an office, the Pastor shall be responsible for cleaning them before leaving.

# Writing a Pastoral Job Description

It is important to draft a Preliminary Job Description at the beginning of the Pastoral Search. A written Job Description helps you and someone else know what is expected of them.

Different people have different ideas of what a job entails. A written Job Description helps clarify the job and can eliminate misunderstandings. It also serves as a standard which can be used for evaluation for the worker and by the authority they answer to. It is a good idea to have a written Job Description for every position of service in your church.

Writing a Job Description should be a process involving someone in authority and the individual considered for the position. The process is pretty much the same in preparing a written Job Description for a Pastor and other workers in a church. There are just a few differences in preparing a Job Description for a Pastor.

If the duties for a Pastor are spelled out in the **Church Constitution & By- Laws**, or **Church Policy Manual**, those duties should be included as part of the Job Description.

## 1.    Write Down the Details of the Job You Want Done.

This is the Preliminary Job Description. Everyone must understand this will be modified and adapted later to align with the Candidate's spiritual gift and abilities, in the context of fulfilling the role of Pastor in your specific church.

The following are some areas to address in a Pastor's Job Description. You need to customize this list for your church. You may want to change some items, eliminate some or add others. Once this *Preliminary Job Description* is drafted, it must be submitted to the Church for further modifications and then for their approval.

1.1. The Pastor shall pray faithfully, and regularly, for all the members and attendees of the Church and for people in the community.

1.2. The Pastor shall study the Word of God: to live it, preach it and teach it.

1.3. The Pastor shall serve as the Shepherd of this Church, providing spiritual food and guidance.

1.4. The Pastor shall attempt to restore the wayward and seek the lost.

1.5. The Pastor shall plan and lead the worship, the teaching, the services, the special meetings and the general church program.
- All teaching materials shall be coordinated with the Pastor.
- All music shall be coordinated with the Pastor to ensure a flow between the message in the sermon and songs.
- He shall prepare an *Annual Proposed Calendar* for the Church.

1.6. The Pastor shall carefully choose and accept responsibility for all speakers and musicians who fill the pulpit.

1.7. The Pastor shall review for possible approval all new ministries and programs proposed for your church.

1.8. The Pastor shall select leaders for the various ministries of your church. Some positions may be subject to Church approval.

1.9. The Pastor shall serve as the executive leader, coordinating the corporate ministry of your church, acting as one of the legal representatives of the Church.

The Trustees, not the Pastor, should execute all legal documents, relating to the physical property or physical assets of the Church.

1.10.   The Pastor shall serve as moderator at all church business meetings.

1.11.   The Pastor shall serve as an ex-officio member of all committees and boards.

1.12.   The Pastor shall interview, hire or approve all ministry related and office staff. The church reserves the right to review any Prospective employee. Any additional Pastoral staff must be approved, first by the Pastor, then the Church Board and then by the Church.

1.13   The Pastor shall administer the ordinances of Believer's Baptism and the Lord's Supper.

1.14.   The Pastor shall prepare an Annual Report, summarizing his activities and the ministries in your church. He shall submit that to the Church for the Annual Meeting.

1.15.   The Pastor shall conduct weddings and funerals for members and attendees of your church.

## 2.   Include the Preliminary Job Description in the Candidate Packet.

Let them know this is a Preliminary Job Description designed to give them an idea of what you are looking for in a Pastor. Let them know this Job Description will be customized with the specific Pastor you call.

## 3.   Meet with the Candidate.

Meeting personally with the Candidate will help both parties get to know each other better and result in a better personalized Job Description.

This will help him get a much better idea of what you are looking for in a Pastor. It will also help you and him see if there can be a good working dynamic between all parties.

Too many Pastoral Search Committees look at beliefs, backgrounds and at preaching and teaching skills and fail to see how well a Candidate can discuss and negotiate details with the people he will be pastoring.

3.1.  Find out about their interests and abilities.

3.2.  Go step-by-step over each item in the Preliminary Job Description. Explain this is the Preliminary Job Description. This will be adapted later to the spiritual gift and abilities of the person filing the position.

3.3.  Let them ask clarifying questions. Have them write down any clarifications or adaptations.

## 4.  Have The Candidate Develop a Personalized Job Description.

Have the Candidate re-write each item, in the Preliminary Job Description, adapted to the context of his own life, focusing on his gift and abilities. He must write down how he sees them applied in the context of your church.

## 5.  Have The Candidate Draft a Standard of Performance.

A Standard of Performance identifies the goals for the Job Description. This answers questions like: *How much time will be given to each duty*, and *What do they expect to accomplish?*

This is an important task. It develops a measurable standard to the Job Description. This will reveal much about a person. Putting this in writing takes philosophy and ideas and applies them practically in the context of your church.

Allow the Candidate enough take to undertake this task prayerfully before he submits his preliminary response. All parties must understand this is a working document, which will need modifications by both parties.

## 6.   Have the Candidate Submit the Personalized Job Description and Standard of Performance for Review.

After the Candidate completes his Personalized Written Job Description and Standard of Performance, have him return a copy to the Secretary of the Pastoral Search Committee.

6.1.   The Secretary should submit a copy to each member of the Committee to review.
Is it realistic?
Did he emphasis the items, which are important to you?
Are there items, which need clarification?

6.2   The Committee should meet to review the document.

6.2.   The Committee should write down its recommendations to discuss with the Candidate.

## 7.   Meet With the Candidate Again – Review What They Wrote & Finalize the Details.

This in person meeting is very important and very practical. This will help both you and the Candidate again see how well you work together. This is a negotiating time.

7.1.   Address any items you wanted clarified.

7.2.   Review the comments and recommendations from your Committee.

7.3.   Determine together if you need to make any modifications. Identify specifically what they are. Determine if you can make those changes to the document at that meeting.

7.4   If necessary, give him time to make modifications and bring them back to you.

7.5    If you cannot come to a consensus this will help you determine this Candidate is not the one who should be your Pastor.

7.6    If you have come to a consensus on this document that is a good sign. Proceed to the next step.

## 8.    Present the Final Job Description and Standard of Performance to the Church for Approval.

Present the final Job Description and Standard of Performance to your church for its approval before voting on extending the final call to the Candidate.

## 9.    Periodically Review the Job Description & Standard of Performance.

If you call the Candidate to serve as your Pastor, remember, the Job Description and Standard of Performance are not cast in stone. This must be flexible and subject to change.

9.1.    Schedule the first evaluation for within the first thirty (30) days. Evaluate and make revisions as needed and present them to the Church for review and approval.

9.2.    Schedule the second evaluation for ninety (90) days. Evaluate and make revisions as needed and present them to the Church for approval.

9.3.    Consider an Annual Evaluation before the Church Annual Meeting.

# How Each Spiritual Gift Might Serve in a Pastoral Ministry

If you accept the teaching, presented briefly in these materials, that our Spiritual Gift is the basic motivating joy God has given to each of us, and that it helps make us who we are, and then you will want to consider how each gift would manifest itself in a Pastoral Ministry. This can be a big help determining what type of Pastor you are seeking and can help you evaluate each Candidate to see how they may fulfill the role as your Pastor.

I highly recommend each member of the Pastoral Search Committee read my book, *Unraveling the Holy Spirit Controversy*, for a more detailed teaching on the Gifts and Ministries.

The Bible teaches our Gift is *who we are*. It is our special part in the body, which God designed for us (Romans 12; 1 Corinthians 12). Some people are hands some are eyes, some are mouths. Our Gift does not change, but our Ministry, which is how we serve, may change.

As we grow in the Lord, and depend more on the Holy Spirit to change us, we will manifest some characteristics of the other Gifts, but that does not change our Gift. Each Gift has its own strengths and weaknesses, which it brings to the ministry. Each one must learn to depend on God to help them. When we learn that principle, it helps us understand and relate to ourselves and each other better. It helps us pray more effectively for each other and help us all minister more effectively together.

The following summary of each Gift are **my Conclusions** about the Spiritual Gifts based on my understanding of **Biblical Principles** and **Personal Observations.** I believe they are correct, but they are not dogma.

As you look at Prospective Candidates you will want to keep in mind their Spiritual Gift will give them a particular perspective on ministry. You need to decide if that perspective is the one you want someone to bring to your Pastorate.

1.  ### The Giver as a Pastor - *The Idea Person*
    (*metadidomi*)   **Romans 12:8**

The word *Giving*, is the translation of the Greek word, **metadidomi**. It means, *one that imparts*. We often think of the Giver as one who gives money because the word *giving* means to **impart**.

This is not limited to imparting money. The person with the Gift of Giving does not just focus on giving money. People with the Gift of Giving find their greatest joy in giving of themselves. They may give their *resources* or give their *ideas*.

○    The Giver's **Joy** is Coming Up with **Ideas, and the Resources** to bring their ideas into reality.

○    Givers are **Creative-Idea people**, but are **often misunderstood** because they are **complex thinkers**.
-    They need to **simplify** what they have to say (Romans 12:8).
-    You have to learn to **listen carefully** to what they say.
     A wise man will be able to discern what they are saying          Proverbs 20:5
-    Though Givers may like people, they tend to **withdraw** because they are often misunderstood.

○    Givers often have **Financial Resources** to give *(unless they have given it all away)*, because their ideas usually work in a secular context.

O   Givers usually do not become a Pastor. If they do, it is usually because Rulers and Exhorters, who are often in leadership positions, are intrigued with their creativity and work so well with them. They usually work best in a larger church with more than one Pastor, or a very active lay leadership.

O   Remember, Givers often come up with an Idea and Resources, but not **How to Implement** them. All seven Gifts must work together.
-   **Rulers** need to help Givers crystallize their ideas into a Big Picture and then help put together the Outline and Plan to make the Ideas happen.
-   **Teachers** fill in the details for the plan.
-   **Prophets** convince others the plan is good.
-   **Mercy People** give the emotional support as people carry out the plan.
-   **Ministry People** do the work.
-   **Exhorters** encourage others and help see the plans are completed.

O   The Giver's greatest source of **frustration** and lack of fulfillment in life comes from two things:
-   People do not understand and/or do not implement their Ideas.
-   People tend to take advantage of their Giving.

O   Givers Usually **Get Along Best With** and **Often Marry** a Ruler or Exhorter.
-   The **Ruler** listens to their ideas and acts on them.
-   The **Exhorter** sees that the Givers ideas are implemented.

O   The Giver's **Areas of Weakness:**
Romans 12:8, tells the Giver to give with simplicity. Givers tend to be too complicated.

If the Giver does not see people acting on their ideas, or using their resources wisely, they have a

127

tendency to shut down, and withhold their ideas and resources.

The Giver may have a tendency to try to use their resources to manipulate people to accept, or to implement their ideas.

○    How Givers **Present the Gospel:**
They tend to focus on the wonderful gift of eternal life God unselfishly gave for us and the opportunity God gives us to share that gift with others.

## 2.    <u>The Ruler as a Pastor</u> - *The Leader*
### *(proistemi)*   **Romans 12:8**

The word *Ruling*, is the translation of the Greek word: **proistemi**. It means, *one that takes the lead*. The person with the Gift of Ruling finds their real joy in keeping the overview. Rulers are usually good at seeing the way things should work.

○    The Ruler's **Joy** is organizing something.

○    Rulers have an uncanny ability to look at an idea, problem, or situation and see the Big Picture.

○    Rulers usually do not see all the details, but get the overview necessary for coming up with an outline for a plan.
-   Remember, they are not detailed people, but they like details because details make their plans work.
-   **Teachers** can help the Ruler by providing the details they need.

○    Rulers can get frustrated if they are not supervising a Project.

- Try not to let them get bogged down in small detail work.

○ Rulers usually become Pastors in churches which need re-organization or in churches with many more people serving. Churches call them more for their organizational focus rather than preaching or counseling.

○ Rulers like to see things go the way they planned.
- Because they can see the *Big Picture*, they believe their plans take into account contingencies others may overlook.
- They can get very frustrated when things do not go the way they planned.
- They often view opposition to their plans as a personal attack.

○ Rulers often try to do it all by themselves, so things will go as they planned.
- This can overwhelm them to where they get discouraged and slack off.
- They need to be diligent about delegating and getting others involved and not try to do it all by themselves.
- Help them by doing your part to help make their plans work.

○ Rulers Usually **Get Along Best With** and **Often Marry** Givers or Teachers.
- The **Giver** gives them ideas which they find challenging to organize.
- The **Teacher** fills in the details to their plans.

○ The Ruler's **Areas of Weakness:**
Romans 12:8, tells the Ruler to rule with diligence. Apparently, Rulers have a tendency to slack off. This may be due to the fact Rulers have a tendency to get bogged down with all that needs to be done. They can get so overwhelmed by all there is to do. Sometimes they try to do it all by themselves. When

they discover they cannot do everything they in turn tend to slack off.

They usually want things to go the way they planned. This causes them to get frustrated with people or things, which interfere with their plans.

They can have a hard time with people who change their plans.

O    How Rulers **Present the Gospel:**
They tend to focus on the concept God has a plan for the ages and a plan for each of our lives. They love the order and organization God can bring to lives.

### 3.    The Teacher as a Pastor - *The Researcher* (*didaskon*)   Romans 12:7

The Greek word: ***didaskon***, translated *teacher,* in our English Bible, comes from the root word, *learner.* A teacher, is one whose greatest joy is learning. In this context it indicates *one who gathers information and then shares it with others.* That does not mean they have to be able to stand up in front of a crowd to do the imparting. Sometimes they do it: in front of a group, by writing, or one on one.

O    The Teacher's **Joy** is gathering information.
-    Help provide them with credible information.

O    Teachers are very detailed people.
-    They love lots of details.
-    They can overwhelm you with details.

O    Information, *The Facts*, are very important to Teachers.
-    They can never have enough information.

- Do not discount the information they provide or they will not give you information you need, when you need it next time.

○ Churches often call Teachers to Pastor after they just had a **Prophet** or **Ruler** as Pastor. Churches usually call them for their knowledge of the Word.

○ Teachers have a hard time being **concise.**
   - Do not have them present a summary.
   - They see all truth as important and have a hard time leaving out details.
   - When they preach, they include a lot of information and speak a long time.

○ Teachers would rather do research and learn, than teach others (Romans 12:7).
   - They have to work on the making sure they give the information they gathered, to others, in a useful way.

○ Teachers are willing to let others teach. They would rather have others do the actual teaching, so they can concentrate on studying.

○ Teachers Usually **Get Along Best With** and **Often Marry** Rulers or Prophets.
   - The **Rulers** give them something to research.
   - The **Prophets** take their information and use it.

○ The Teacher's **Areas of Weakness:**
   Romans 12:7, tells the Teacher to teach. Too often Teachers will study and accumulate information, but will not share it with others.

   The Teacher has to beware their accumulation of information does not make them think they are better than other people. They sometimes have a tendency to get puffed up and talk down to others.

   They have a tendency to give a person more information than they want.

○ How Teachers **Present the Gospel:**
They tend to focus on the overwhelming body of evidence, which supports the Scriptures. They are fascinated at all the information in the Bible. They tend to try to present the whole plan of God, from Genesis to Revelation, in one sitting. They have a hard time leaving out details.

## 4. <u>The Prophet as a Pastor</u>
### *The Persuader (propheteia)* **Romans 12:6**

The word Prophet, in this context, takes on its basic meaning of *one who proclaims the truth.*

The Prophet focuses on logic, and is concerned about right and wrong. This person can usually identify if something is wrong *(small or large)*, and comes up with a solution to correct it, even if the solution is not completely thought out.

○ The Prophet's **Joy** is identifying right & wrong and persuading others.

○ Prophets see everything as right or wrong, logical or illogical.
- They do not see *gray areas.*
- They need information.
- **Teachers** can provide them the details they need.
- **Mercy People** comfort the people Prophets hurt with their directness.

○ Prophets usually have something to say.
- When they see something they think is right or wrong, no matter how small or insignificant it may seem to others, they have to point it out.
- What they say tends to be blunt.

○ Prophets like being Pastors so they can have a platform to persuade others. They often preach powerful, convincing messages. They tend to use *persuasion* more than information in their teaching and preaching.

○ Prophets are usually very intense.
  - They can easily offend or irritate others.
  - Try to understand where they are coming from.

○ Prophets may seem arrogant because of their outspoken opinions.
  - They believe very strongly in what they say.
  - They are often critical of what they think is wrong.
  - Listen carefully to what they say.
  - If you believe they are wrong, do not attack their position or logic, they view that as a personal attack. Present your stand as another viewpoint and ask them to take time and evaluate it for you.

○ Prophets can be very effective convincing others of their viewpoint.

○ Prophets like to debate but they are not good listeners.

○ Prophets are very dedicated to what they believe is right.
  - This often drives them to political involvement.

○ Sometimes, Prophets may be willing to sacrifice presenting certain details *(facts, truth)* if the other information seems illogical to them.

○ Prophets often need help with People Skills.

○ Prophets Usually **Get Along Best With** and **Often Marry** Teachers or Mercy People.
  - **Teachers** give them the information they need.
  - **Mercy** people help buffer them. Sometimes those are the only one who will marry them.

○    The Prophet's **Areas of Weakness:**
Romans 12:6, tells the Prophet to prophesy according to the proportion of faith. Prophets tend to either hold back, or go too far.

Prophets have the tendency to get indignant when others do not respond to what they think is the truth.

They tend to react too quickly to what they view as opposition to truth.

They have to be careful they do not tear people down. They need to make sure they are not insensitive, as they seek to persuade people to change.

They can be a good people person, but they have to work hard at it.

○    How Prophets **Present the Gospel:**
They tend to focus on the truth of the Gospel. They seek to convince others it is the only truth.

## 5.    The Mercy Person as a Pastor
*The Comforter* (*eleeo*)
**Romans 12:8**

The word *Mercy*, is the translation of the Greek word: ***eleeo***. It means *to withhold something negative, which someone deserves.*

The person with the Gift of Mercy is a **comforter**, *someone who does not want to see people suffer*. They are concerned about people's feelings.

○    The Mercy Person often views people as victims. They are even willing to show mercy to those whom others do not believe deserve mercy.

○    They love to see a person's emotional needs met.

O    The person with the Gift of Mercy helps to create an atmosphere for service.

O    The Mercy Person's **Joy** is comforting people & seeing needs are met.

O    They are very good at the shepherding aspects of the Pastorate.

O    One of the Mercy Person's greatest motivations is to see people comforted.
-    They often go out of their way to help others.
-    They will sacrifice their own comfort or needs to help others.
-    They like to let people know God is the Ultimate Comforter.

O    They want to see people get practical help, which makes people feel good.
-    Does your church have a practical way of showing people God's love?

O    Mercy People often look at people as victims, when things go bad.
-    They have a tendency to overlook people's faults.
-    They believe there is good in everyone, even in **Prophets**.

O    Mercy People tend to get too involved in other people's problems.
-    That can lead them to despair.
-    That can lead then to lose their joy.
-    Try to bring cheer to them (Romans 12:8).

O    They do not like those who seem insensitive to other people's feelings.

O    Mercy People can be cruel to those they think do not deserve mercy because of those other people's actions or attitudes to others.

○ Mercy People may be willing to sacrifice truth, in order to help others.

○ Mercy People Usually **Get Along Best With** and **Often Marry** Prophets or Ministry People/Doers.
   - The **Prophet** greatly needs them to attain balance in life.
   - The **Ministry People/Doers** are active and need their comfort.

○ The Mercy Person's **Areas of Weakness:**
   Romans 12:8, tells the Mercy Person to be more cheerful. Mercy People tend to get moody and depressed too easily.

   The Person with the Gift of Mercy, tends to get too involved in other people's problems and feelings, and sometimes breaks down under the load.

   Surprisingly, they can be very unmerciful with a person they believe does not care about others.

○ How Mercy People **Present the Gospel:**
   They tend to focus on the love and mercy of God. They try to help people see God is Love and we need His help to love others more effectively.

## 6. The Ministry People/Doers as a Pastor
*The Server, The Doer (diakonia)* **Romans 12:7**

The word *Ministry*, is the translation of the Greek word: ***diakonia***. Ministry is one of those words, which has different shades of meaning, determined by its context.

The person with the Gift of Ministry, is *one whose real joy comes from doing practical things for others.* They are the *Ultimate Servers.* If there is a job to do, this person will usually be there to get it done.

I refer to them as the **Doer** because they love to be active doing a task.

○ The Doer's **Joy** is Doing a Job.

○ The Doer has more joy *doing* a Job, than *completing* it.
- They will always be doing something.

○ Doers are often Not Initiators.
- Some will not volunteer for a job but would gladly do a job if you asked.

○ Doers usually are not Public Speakers.
- They would usually rather do a job than speak in front of others, so they often do not seek to become Pastors because of the pulpit ministry.
- They will speak if they feel it is necessary to help them do a job.

○ Some churches call Doers as Pastors because they are good workers. They can make good Pastors in small churches where a Pastor had many extra duties.

○ Doers are detailed people.
- They want, and need, to know specifically what to do.
- They need to be provided with a specific job to do.

○ Doers have a tendency to get sidetracked by details on a job.
- They can spend hours on the details and not end up completing the job.
- Their joy is *doing*, not *completing*.
- They need a specific Job Description or List of Things to Do.

○ Doers are not afraid of work.
- They are willing to get their hands dirty.

○ Doers are usually very dependable people.

○ Doers want to know what they are doing is important.
- They do not work for recognition but like to know, what they do is appreciated.
- Recognize their work.

○ Doers Usually **Get Along Best With** and **Often Marry** Mercy People or Exhorters.
- The **Mercy** Person comforts them and sees their needs are met.
- The **Exhorter** encourages them and motivates them to complete a job.

○ The Doer's **Areas of Weakness:**
Romans 12:7, tells the Doer to, *wait on our ministering.* They are exhorted to stick with the job they are supposed to be doing. Being such detailed people, Doers have a tendency to get sidetracked by the many details they encounter in a job.

The Doer seems to have the tendency to do too much and to focus on the job rather than on people.

If they feel they are doing too much, and not appreciated, they will often close down and stop doing anything for a while.

○ How Doers **Present the Gospel:**
They tend to focus on the idea God has a special place of service for people and their service can make a difference.

## 7. **The Exhorter as a Pastor**
*The Encourager (parakaleo)*
**Romans 12:8**

The word *Exhortation*, is the translation of the Greek word: **parakaleo**. It means *one called alongside to help or encourage.*

The Exhorter, is *one whose greatest joy is stimulating the faith of others.* The Exhorter wants to see *people encouraged* and *a job completed.*

○   The Exhorters **Joy** is Encouraging Others so a Job gets completed.

○   Many people like Exhorters because they encourage people and as a result things get done. They are often called as Pastors.

○   Exhorters are very results oriented.
    -   They are the **Completer**.
    -   They are the one who will see a job is completed.
    -   They can **motivate** others to do a job.
    -   They will do a job themselves if they have to.

○   Exhorters are almost always **saying something**.
    -   They have to open their mouth to encourage or motivate others.
    -   They often give advice to help others, even if they are not asked.
    -   Though most people like their encouragement, people do not want to be encouraged all the time.

○   Exhorters are almost always **doing something**.
    -   Unlike the **Server**, they are doing a job to complete it. Their focus is on the end, not the moment.
    -   They enjoy the movement toward a goal, but often miss the joy in the journey.
    -   When a job is completed they need another project to complete.

○   Exhorters often look for better ways to get a job done.

○   Exhorters can get very discouraged if they do not see results.

- If they do not see others completing a job, they stop encouraging others and try to do it themselves (Romans 12:8). This can cause them to burn out.
- Try to encourage the Encourager.
- **Servers** can be the biggest help to them, as Servers accomplish a job.
- **Givers** are a real help because they provide the ideas and resources to complete a job.

○ Exhorters Usually **Get Along Best With** and **Often Marry** Doers or Givers.
  - The **Doers** respond to their encouragement and complete a job.
  - The **Giver** likes the fact the Exhorter completes things so they give more ideas and resources.

○ The Exhorter's **Areas of Weakness:**
Romans 12:8, tells the Exhorter to exhort. Exhorters are like Doers, they have a tendency to get sidetracked.

Instead of encouraging others, they get involved doing the job. They need to train and encourage others instead of doing the job themselves.

The person with the Gift of Exhortation, especially as a Pastor, has a tendency to do more than they should in their quest to encourage others and to get the job done.

The Exhorter feels they must always be moving toward a goal. Sometimes they do not enjoy their successes because they are pressing on too hard.

They have a tendency to run down and wear out.

○ How the Exhorter **Presents the Gospel**:
They tend to focus on the completeness we can find in Christ and how He helps us accomplish meaningful things in life, which will be rewarded in the end.

# The Installation Service
## *When the Candidate Officially Becomes the Pastor*

An Installation Service is a time of celebration as well as a very solemn occasion. This is the time when your church officially installs the Candidate as your Pastor. It is very much like a Wedding Ceremony with the exchange of solemn vows.

Just as in a Wedding, though a couple may love each other before they are married, and though they may be engaged and set a wedding date, they are not legally married until they make their vows and are officially pronounced husband and wife. In the same way, the Candidate does not officially become the Pastor until the completion of the vows and the Installation Service.

Schedule this service at a time when people from your church and from surrounding churches can attend so they can celebrate with you. It is usually best to schedule this for a Saturday or Sunday Afternoon. It is always a nice touch to have an *Installation Reception* immediately following the service.

You will notice the suggested service contains two brief biblical challenges. These are not full sermons. Though you should clearly present the Word of God, the purpose of this service is to install your new Pastor, not to preach a sermon. I recommend you do not make this a long service. It should be similar in length to a wedding.

In this section, you will notice the person you have called as Pastor is still called the Candidate. They are not officially the Pastor until the after the vows.

## Participants & Invitees

The Pastoral Installation Service is a time of celebration and a good opportunity to invite as many people as possible from your church and community to attend.

## 1.  Invitees.

- All Your Church Members & Attendees.
- Other Churches & Ministers Your Church Fellowship With.
- Other Churches and Ministers in Your Area.
- Local Dignitaries and Elected Officials.
- Local Media.
  The installation of a Pastor is a news worthy event. It is a good opportunity for local news to become acquainted with your new Pastor.
- The General Public.
  Some people in your area, who are looking for a church, will attend if invited.

## 2.  Participants,

- The Candidate and His Family.
- Pastoral Search Committee Members.
- Church Staff & Church Officers.
- Officiating Minister.
- Musicians.

## Suggested Order of Service

This Suggested Order of Service will work for both a small or large church. Prayerfully consider including the various elements suggested here. Feel free to make any changes you desire.

Have the Candidate and his family sit in one of the front rows of the church. Other people participating in the service should also be seated in a front row or on the platform.

I recommend having guest Pastors or Ministers sit in the front, though that is optional, especially if they came with people from their church.

It is a nice idea to have a *Guest Book* for everyone to sign. It is also nice to have *Bulletins* with an Order of Service.

Suggested words and vows for the participants are provided here in italics. Those words may be used exactly as written *(some participants will greatly appreciate having these provided)*. You may decide to change any of the words or have participants speak extemporaneously.

## 1.　Background Music

Have some nice friendly background instrumental music playing starting at least 10 minutes before the service. Music helps set the mood.

## 2.　Opening Song

A good opening song sets the tone for the rest of the service. This is the call to begin the service. This is not the official formal welcome but a way to bring everyone together.

**Two Ways to Do This.**

**O　Have Someone Lead the Opening Song.**

The song leader should approach the pulpit, smile and invite the people to sing along. The words to the song should be available in a hymnal, songbook, song sheet or projected.

If you want to use a hymn, a good old hymn for this occasion is, *To God Be the Glory.*

Suggested words of greeting before the song (keep it short):

*Welcome! Please stand and sing with me as we begin this joyous occasion with [Name of Song]*

**O　Have a Nice Uplifting Special Number.**

Another nice way to start this service is with a nice uplifting special number. This can be done by a soloist, small group, choir or DVD. Make sure the song has a good instrumental introduction to signal people the service has begun. The singer(s) may invite the Congregation to stand and sing after the first verse, or on a closing chorus.

## 3. Welcome

After the Opening Song is finished, it is time for the formal welcome. The Chairman of the Pastoral Search Committee should issue this welcome.

> *On behalf of [Name of Church] we would like to welcome you to this special Pastoral Installation Service. We are honored you came. Today we will be conducting the formal installation of [Name] to serve as the Pastor of [Name of Church].*

At this time it is a nice idea to ask any ministers present to stand and have them introduce themselves.

> *We would like to ask any visiting ministers to please stand and introduce themselves.*

After introducing visiting ministers, be sure to welcome any local dignitaries or elected officials.

> *We are also honored to have some of our local dignitaries in attendance today. [Mention each one by name].*

After introducing the ministers and local dignitaries, invite the people to stand and introduce the person who will be offering the Opening Prayer.

> *Would you please stand with me as [Name], [Name of Their Church Office] comes to open this service in prayer.*

## 4. Opening Prayer

The Opening Prayer should be offered by a Senior Church Officer, such as the Chairman of your Board of Deacons.

Please do not read the following, prayer. It is only provided as an example:

> *Heavenly Father, we are so grateful to have a loving God like you. We ask for your presence to be with us in a special way and we ask for your blessing to be on this service. We thank you for leading us in our*

*search for a Pastor and are so grateful you brought [Name] and his family to come serve as our Pastor. May everything we say and do in this service bring honor and glory to you. We ask this in the precious name of Jesus, Amen.*

## 5. Optional Congregational Song

If you are a musical church, and your people like to sing, this is a nice time for another congregational song.

The way to do this is, as soon as the Opening Prayer is completed, the person, or group, which will be leading the song, should come immediately to the pulpit and invite the Congregation to remain standing and sing along.

*Please remain standing me and join us as we sing [Name of Song].*

## 6. Report from Pastoral Search Committee & Introduction of the Candidate & His Family

Someone from the Pastoral Search Committee should come to the pulpit, introduce themselves and provide a brief report to let people know a through procedure was followed to select this Pastor.

*My name is [Name], I served as [Role] on the Pastoral Search Committee. Our committee was formed on [Date] by this church, and charged with the solemn responsibility of helping our church find a new Pastor. We looked at various recommendations, made contacts and interviewed various Prospective Candidates. After much prayerful and careful deliberation, we recommended our church consider [Name] to serve as our Pastor. After the people in our church had to opportunity to meet [Name] and his family, and after they had the opportunity to hear him preach, and to ask him questions. Our church choose to extend the call to [Name] to serve as our Pastor.*

*It is now my honor to introduce to you [Name] and his family.*

Motion to the Candidate and his family come to the front of the church.

Ask the Candidate to introduce his family members. When he is done doing this, invite the Officiating Minister, who will be issuing the Charge, to come to the pulpit, while the Candidate and his family remain standing in front of the Congregation.

## 7.    The Charge

### 7.1    Charge to the Candidate

The Officiating Minister issues a brief Biblical Charge to the Candidate. This includes summarizing the God given duties and responsibilities of a Pastor. This is similar to the charge a Pastor issues to a couple about to be married. Do this while the Candidate and his family are standing.

### 7.2    The Charge to the Church

The same Minister *(or another pastor)* should then issue a Biblical charge to the Church Leadership and Congregation. This includes reminding them of their responsibilities of a congregation to the Pastor.

## 8.    The Vows

This is the point in the service when the vows are made. This is similar to Wedding Vows. In a wedding the Bride and the Groom exchange vows. A newer trend in some weddings is to include additional vows from other family members and, in some cases a vow from all of the people present to help and encourage the couple.

The Pastor Installation Vows include vows, not just from the Pastor but also from his Family, the Church Leaders, the Congregation and Others attending. This gives everyone a part in the service. It emphasizes the solemnity of the occasion as well as helps to make it more meaningful and memorable.

The Officiating Minister, or another Pastor *(if you have a number of Pastors present, whom you would like to have involved in the service)*, can issue the different vows.

If more than one Minister is involved, they should come to the pulpit for their portion of the vows, being introduced by the Minister who participates before them.

### 8.1.  Minister addresses the Candidate

*[Name] realizing the solemnity of the vows we are about to make, If you are willing to make the commitment before God and this assembly to serve as Pastor of [Name of Church], please step forward.*

Candidate takes one step forward.

*Do you [Name] pledge, to the best of your ability and with God's help, to faithfully fulfill all the duties of Pastor of [Name of Church]?*

The Candidate responds: *I do.*

### 8.2.  Minister addresses the Candidate's Family

*[Name each member of the Candidate's Family] If it is your desire to support your [Husband, Father, Grandfather, etc.] in his decision to accept the Pastorate of this church, will you step forward and join him?*

Family steps forward and joins the Candidate.

*Do you pledge, to the best of your ability and with God's help to pray for and encourage your [Husband, Father, Grandfather, etc.] as he seeks to fulfill the duties God has entrusted to Him as Pastor of [Name of Church]?*

Each Family members responds together: *I do.*

### 8.3.  Minister addresses the Church Leadership

*If you are an elected officer or leader of any ministry in this church, and if it is your desire to assist your new Pastor and help him as he seeks to fulfill the call God has given him to serve as Pastor of this church, will you come forward?*

Church leaders step forward and join the Candidate.

*Do you pledge, to the best of your ability and with God's help, to pray for, encourage and work together with [name of Pastor] as he seeks to fulfill the duties God has entrusted to him as Pastor of [Name of Church]?*

Each Leader responds together: *I do.*

### 8.4. The Minister addresses the Church Members

*If you are a Member of this church and if it is your desire to see God's blessing rest upon this church and on your new Pastor will you please stand where you are.*

Members respond by standing where they are.

*Do you, Members of [Name of Church] pledge, to the best of your ability and with God's help, to faithfully pray for Pastor [Name] and his family, as they seek to honor and glorify God? And do you pledge to do whatever you can to advance the cause of Christ through this church?*

Each Member responds together: *I do.*

### 8.5. The Minister addresses the Attendees

*Honored Guests and each of you attending this service, if it is your desire to see God's hand of blessing rest upon [Name of Church] and their New Pastor [Name], will you please stand.*

Attendees respond by standing where they are.

*Do you pledge, to the best of your ability and with God's help, to encourage Pastor [Name] and the good people here at [Name of Church] as they seek to honor God, by spreading His love in this church and in your community?*

Each Attendee responds together: *I do.*

148

## 9.    The Blessing

### 9.1.    Blessing for the Pastor & His Family

The Officiating Minister calls upon other Pastors and the Church Leadership, who are already at the front of the church, to lay hands on the Pastor and his family to confer a Blessing.

Have at least one Minister and Two Church Leaders Pray *(if your church allows women to pray in public meetings, consider having one of the people praying be a women)*

### 9.2.    Blessing for the Church

After the Blessing of the Pastor and his family. The Officiating Minister calls upon everyone present to join hands for a Blessing for the Church.

Have at least one Minister and Two Church Leaders Pray.

## 10.    The Presentation

After the Blessing, the Officiating Minister will make the announcement introducing the New Pastor of your church.

*Pastor [Name] and your family, will you please come to the podium.*

The Pastor and his family come to the Podium.

*It is my honor to present to you, Pastor [Name] and his family.*

Pause for Response from the Congregation

*Pastor [Name], as your first official duty as Pastor of [Name of Church] will you closes this service in prayer?*

## 11.    Closing Prayer

The Closing Prayer is led by the new Pastor. This is his first official action as Pastor.

## 12.   Closing Music

The instrumentalists (no vocalists), shall play an uplifting song as the Pastor and his family form a Reception Line and begin to greet people. The Closing Music should continue for about 10 minutes or until the Reception Line is finished.

## The Installation Reception

An Installation Reception welcoming the New Pastor and His Family should be held as a celebration capstone following the Pastoral Installation Service.

If your church has a fellowship hall, that would be the best place for the Reception.

The Reception could be nice refreshments or a buffet meal. You can have it catered or you can have people from your church and other churches bring food.

It is a nice touch to either have recorded music or to have some musicians playing during the reception.

The Reception should last about an hour.

# Resources for Finding Prospective Pastoral Candidates

One of the greatest challenges facing a Pastoral Search Committee is locating good Prospective Candidates. Many people will recommend names to you, but good Prospective Candidates are hard to find.

Be sure to inform your church, as well as each resource you contact, about your policy to require a written **Prospective Pastoral Candidate Recommendation Form** in advance.

If you or anyone on your Pastoral Search Committee knows of someone specific you would like to consider as a candidate, ask someone to submit a **Prospective Pastoral Candidate Recommendation Form**.

Many time churches contact former Guest Speakers to become Prospective Candidates. Be sure someone submits a **Prospective Pastoral Candidate Recommendation Form** for them before you consider them.

## 1.  Pastors, Occupational Ministry People or Missionaries You Know.

Those in Occupational Christian Ministry are often one of the best sources for Prospective Candidates.

Contact Pastors and other people in occupational Christian Ministry your church knows. Those people are familiar with your church. Ask them if they will prayerfully consider recommending someone as a Prospective Candidate for your church.

## 2.  Church or Pastor's Fellowships.

Is your church part of a fellowship of churches or a part of an association? If so, that is another good source for contacts. They often have some familiarity with your church or area and may be familiar with some good prospects who may be interested in Pastoring in your area. Let them know you are looking for recommendations for Prospective Candidates.

## 3.    Bible Schools or Seminaries.

Do you have Bible Schools or Seminaries you support or endorse? Most schools maintain a Christian Service Placement Office to help match their graduates and alumni with service opportunities. Let them know you are only looking for alumni to consider as Prospective Candidates, not recent graduates with no Pastoral experience.

## 4.    Mission Boards.

Mission Boards, with whom you have a working relationship, can be a good source for Prospective Candidates. They often know of Pastors from churches, who support their ministry, who are looking for a church. They may also have missionaries returning from the field or some seeking a Pastorate, or applicants they believe may be a better match for you than for their ministry.

## 5.    Printed & Online Resources.

Some churches go as far as to place a classified ad in ministry publications they subscribe to and trust. Make sure your ad states your policy of requiring someone, other than a Prospective Candidate, to submit a **Prospective Pastoral Candidate Recommendation Form**. Otherwise, a Potential Candidate may eliminate himself by submitting his own name.

# Customizing & Using Forms

Specific forms, to accompany the manual, which preceded this book, were designed to help churches in their search for the Right Pastor. A number of churches used those forms successfully over the years.

Such forms would not be helpful in this book format, so instead the explanation of each form is provided here. You can develop your own, or you can download the forms online, in MS-Word format. This enables you to download those forms and customize them for your unique situation. You may also contact Challenge International or the author to request any of these forms by email.

Just like this book, the forms are quite detailed. You should customize each form but are encouraged to be careful what you remove. Though you may not have a stand on certain issues, and may not have certain ministries, mentioned in a form, most Prospective Pastors have a position and idea about this issues or ministries. It is best to learn their position before you extend a call to them, even if those items do not seem important to you ate the moment. That would be much better than discovering later you have significant differences.

These forms are for use by the Pastoral Search Committee. Each of these forms should be customized for your specific church and then submitted to your church for approval. It may be advantageous to email the forms to the parties involved. That enables someone to answer questions in electronic format, which will be easier to distribute to the Committee members later for review.

## 1.     Candidating Procedure Checklist

The **Candidate Procedure Checklist** provides a step-by-step checklist to assist the Pastoral Search Committee in the process of fulfilling their task. You must customize this procedure and checklist.

Use a separate **Candidate Procedure Checklist** to track the progress for each Candidate.

## 2. Pastoral Qualifications Review

A **Pastoral Qualifications Review Form** helps make sure a Candidate meets the qualifications important to your church. Customize this form.

## 3. Principles & Practices Checklist

The **Principles & Practices Checklist** identifies the principles and policies important to your church, which you use in the interview process. Customize this form.

## 4. Prospective Pastoral Candidate Recommendation Form

You should require someone to complete and submit a **Prospective Candidate Recommendation Form** before you consider any Candidate. Customize this form.

## 5. Pastoral Candidate Questionnaire

The **Pastoral Candidate Questionnaire** asks the Candidate about each of the qualifications listed on your **Pastoral Qualifications Review**. Be sure to include each item on your **Principles and Practices Worksheet** and ask them to state their position. Let them know you do not have a position on some of the items addressed on this form, but realize some Pastors do. Let them know, a *No Position* response to a question is acceptable. Customize this form.

Send this form to the Candidate with a request to return it to the committee within two weeks.

The information on this form is confidential and is only for use by the Pastoral Search Committee.

## 6. Pastoral Candidate Reference Form

A **Pastoral Candidate Reference Form** should be sent by the Pastoral Search Committee to the people provided as references by the Candidate, with instructions to return them directly to the Pastoral Search Committee.

Let them know these forms shall remain confidential and the fact the Candidate will never be allowed to see these. Customize this form.

Additional **Pastoral Candidate Reference Forms** should be sent, by the Pastoral Search Committee, to the additional three (3) names provided by those filling out the reference forms. That means, unless there is duplication *(which is possible)*, you will be sending out nine (9) additional reference forms.


*May God bless you with His wisdom*
*as you undertake this task for Him* (James 1:5)

# About the Author Dr. Larry A. Maxwell

Dr. Larry A. Maxwell attended Practical Bible Training School *(now Davis College)* in Johnson City, New York and Lynchburg Baptist College *(now Liberty University)* in Lynchburg, Virginia, where he majored in Pastoral Studies. He later graduated from the India Theological Seminary in Brahmavar, India, with both a Masters and Doctorate in Biblical Studies.

He was ordained to the Gospel Ministry in 1976, by his Pastor, Dr. Jerry Falwell and *Thomas Road Baptist Church* in Lynchburg, Virginia, where he was a member. He has served as a Church Planter, Youth Pastor, Pastor and was listed as Associate Evangelist, under Dr. John R. Rice with *The Sword of the Lord.*

Dr. Maxwell founded *Challenge International* in 1981, to help *Challenge Others to Greater Service for Christ.* He has served as an advisor to Pastors, Church Boards and other organizations.

He teaches on both the undergraduate and graduate level. He served as Academic Dean of the *Colonial Hills Baptist College* and of *The India Theological Seminary International Extension.*

He is a popular conference speaker and award-winning author. Some of his books include:

○    Gaining Personal Financial Freedom, through the Biblical Principles of Finances

○    Gaining Financial Freedom Budget Workbook

- More Than 500 Proven Ways to Reduce Expenses
- Becoming a Dynamic Youth Leader
- 175 Ways to Fund Your Youth Ministry
- You Can Start a Local Church Bible Institute
- The Round Up – Vacation Bible School Manual
- Unraveling the Holy Spirit Controversy

To contact Dr. Maxwell with questions or to schedule him for a consultation or to speak, go to his website: LarryMaxwell.com

# Index

160

Faith Promise ... 67
*Falwell, Jonathan* ... 63
Family Devotions ... 64
Feed the Flock ... 31, 39
Feeding Candidates ... 108-109
Feeding Guest Speakers ... 106-107
Family Life ... 87-88
Family of God ... 48-49
Fellowship ... 19, 57, 58, 60-61
Filling the Pulpit ... 17-19, 27, 52, 92, 120
Films ... 62, 88
Filthy Lucre ... 34, 38
Final Job Description ... 102, 124
Financial Compensation ... 18, 27, 78-79, 94, 97, 102, 105-106, 110-115
Financial Considerations ... 105-117
Financial Policies ... 70
First Date ... 12-13
Firstfruits ... 71
*Focus on the Family* ... 77
Forming Search Committee ... 17, 20
Forms ... 153-155
Fund Raising ... 71
Funding Search Committee ... 105
Funerals ... 20, 76, 121
Gainsayers ... 39
Gambling ... 50
*General Association of Regular Baptist Churches* ... 63
Getting Engaged ... 14
*Gideons* ... 65
Gift of Teaching ... 34, 85-87
Gifts of the Holy Spirit ... 48, 83, 85-87, 125-140
*Girl Scouts* ... 56
Giver ... 83, 126-129, 140
Giver as Pastor ... 126-128
Goals ... 89, 111, 122
*Good News Clubs* ... 56

Google Image Search ... 97
Government Regulations ... 72
Grammatical Historical ... 112
Great Commandment ... 77
Great Commission ... 66, 77
Greedy ... 77
Greek Orthodox ... 45
**Greek Words:**
  *agios* ... 38
  *agnoein* ... 85
  *aischrokerdes* ... 34
  *amachos* ... 35
  *andra* ... 33
  *anipilepton* ... 32
  *aphilarguros* ... 35
  *authade* ... 37
  *chara* ... 86
  *charismaton* ... 86
  *dao* ... 85
  *diakonia* ... 136
  *didaktikon* ... 34
  *didasko* ... 85
  *didaskon* ... 130
  *dikaion* ... 38
  *egkrate* ... 39
  *eleeo* ... 134
  *epieike* ... 162
  *episcope* ... 31
  *gunaikos* ... 33
  *kosmion* ... 33
  *macho* ... 35
  *me* ... 34-37
  *metadidomi* ... 126
  *mias* ... 33
  *nephaleon* ... 33
  *neophuton* ... 36
  *orgilos* ... 37
  *osios* ... 38
  *parakaleo* ... 138
  *paroinon* ... 34
  *philagathon* ... 38
  *philo* ... 33
  *philoxenos* ... 33
  *plekten* ... 34
  *pneuma* ... 64
  *pneumatikon* ... 85

Recommendation Form ... 12, 26, 91, 151-152, 154
Recommendation to Church ... 21, 99-100
Recovery Ministry ... 69
*Red Cross* ... 78
Reference Form ... 93, 96, 154-155
References ... 22, 30, 94-97, 105, 154
References, Additional ... 96
References, Contact ... 22, 94-96
Reformed ... 41, 45
Reimbursement Policy ... 105, 113
Remarriage ... 33, 74-75
Researcher ... 110, 130
Resources ... 83, 126-128, 140, 151-152
Results ... 95, 98, 103, 139
Results (Manifestations) ... 82-85
Retirement ... 20, 27, 79, 112
Retreats ... 57-58, 61
Return of Christ ... 45-46
Revelation ... 45, 132
Review ... 19, 25-28, 31, 42, 67, 74, 79, 81, 94-95, 97-99, 106, 111, 120-121, 123-124, 153-154
Revival Meetings ... 62
Roman Catholic ... 45, 48, 77, 166
Romantic Parallel ... 11-15, 92
*Royal Rangers* ... 56
Ruler ... 83, 127, 128-130, 131
Ruler as Pastor ... 128-130
Rules Own House ... 131-132
Sabbatical ... 35, 79-80
Salary ... 20, 27, 78-79, 102, 107-108, 110-111, 113, 115, 116-117
*Samaritan's Purse* ... 66
Same Sex Marriage ... 74, 78
Satan ... 36
Satellite TV ... 50

Schedule ... 98, 100-103, 124, 121
Schedule, Personal ... 78, 88
Schedule Installation Service ... 103, 141
Secular Humanism ... 77
Secretarial Staff ... 74
Secretary ... 22, 123
Second Coming ... 45-46
Self-Willed ... 37
Seminary ... 89. 152
Senior Citizens ... 21, 59
Server ... 136-140
Server as Pastor ... 136-138
Service Projects ... 58
Severance Policy ... 28, 115-117
Severe Termination ... 116
Shepherd ... 19, 31, 39, 120, 135
Short Term Missions ... 58
Shut-Ins ... 59
Singing Groups ... 57-58, 108
Singles ... 21, 59
Situational ethics ... 34
Slacks on Women ... 42, 50
Sober ... 33, 38
Social Issues ... 78
Social Media ... 6, 73, 97
Song Selection ... 53-54, 120
Song Leader ... 53
Soteriology ... 46-47
Small Groups ... 51, 63, 67
Soul ... 64-65, 87
Soul-Winning ... 62, 87
Sound Doctrine ... 39
Sound System ... 52-53
Sound Tracks ... 42, 53, 90
*Southern Baptist* ... 48-49, 66, 78
Specific Policies to Consider ... 24, 26, 115
Special Business Meeting ... 100, 102
Special Offerings ... 72
Special Music ... 53-54

Wine ... 33-34, 38, 70
Women's Prayer ... 59, 149
*Word of Life Clubs* ... 56-57, 65
World Evangelism ... 49
Worship ... 23, 51-54, 64, 71, 120
Worship Leader ... 53, 120
Worship Ministry ... 51-53, 64
Worship Service ... 23-24, 51-54
Worship Team ... 53

Written Recommendation ... 26, 151
Written Reply ... 94
Writing a Job Description .. 119, 123, 168
*Youth for Christ* ... 57
Young Peoples ... 57
Youth Leader ... 58, 158
Youth Ministry ... 57-58, 66, 90, 158

# Scripture Index
## Indexed Alphabetically by Book

Made in the USA
Middletown, DE
01 August 2017